Creating Leadership

Creating Leadership

How to Change Hippos into Gazelles

Philip Goodwin
Tony Page

BEP BUSINESS EXPERT PRESS

Creating Leadership: How to Change Hippos into Gazelles
Copyright © Business Expert Press, LLC, 2018.

First published in 2018 by
Business Expert Press, LLC
222 East 46th Street, New York, NY 10017
www.businessexpertpress.com

ISBN-13: 978-1-94744-118-7 (paperback)
ISBN-13: 978-1-94744-119-4 (e-book)

Business Expert Press Human Resource Management and Organizational Behavior Collection

Collection ISSN: 1946-5637 (print)
Collection ISSN: 1946-5645 (electronic)

Cover and interior design by S4Carlisle Publishing Services Private Ltd., Chennai, India

First edition: 2018

10 9 8 7 6 5 4 3 2 1

Printed in the United States of America.

Abstract

This informative and inspirational handbook describes how to successfully lead mergers and change in complex organizations. Drawing on a real-life experience, the authors share their insights on how leaders can deliver sustainable change by growing the capacity of everyone within an organization to deliver performance gains, behave like a leader, and encourage leadership in others.

It is a book by practitioners for practitioners telling the real-life story of a leader and a facilitator working together in the complex reality of a multinational organization. It deepens this insight by drawing on a wealth of wider research by academics and leadership practitioners.

Here you will find immediately useable tools, easy to relate to real-life examples, and a little bit of magic in the form of a fable that will sustain you and your colleagues through the twists and turns of what is certain to become an intensely human journey.

Keywords

change, facilitation, leadership, merger, tools, transformation

Contents

Acknowledgments

- The leadership team and staff (past and present) in British Council's East and West Africa Regions. It was an inspiration to work with them. We hope we have done justice to their dedication, creativity, and passion.
- The team members who kindly agreed to be interviewed for the book.
- Wendy Mitchell and RDSi, the qualitative market research company in London, who conducted the field interviews.
- Andy Phillips and Peter Masaaba who did so much of the research with staff that made the breakthrough in Lagos possible.
- Ben Parker who brought his special clarity and big energy on the journey with us from Nairobi to Dar es Salaam (with several other stops on the way).
- Barry Curnow and the Brainstrust participants at CASS Business School in London to whom, one Tuesday evening in October 2007, we first presented an early version of these tales from Africa.
- Harriet Stanes who provided the fine illustrations and Wilson Page who provided graphic design and layout skills.
- Jeremy Keeley and the Sadler Heath organization whose members explored and tested the concepts.
- Bob McKenzie and Vicky Costick at the *Organisations & People Journal* who edited and published a short form of this story.
- The whole team at BEP for turning our manuscript into the fine book now before you.

PART 1

The Challenge

Hippo collapsed foreground; gazelles background

CHAPTER 1

Why Must Leaders Create Leaders?

In October 2015, the government of Hungary decided to close its borders. It was an attempt to stop the inflow from neighboring Croatia of refugees fleeing the war in Syria. In response, the government of Croatia redirected the flow of refugees westward toward Slovenia. By closing borders and redirecting the flow, both countries were pushing the challenge presented by this mass movement of people somewhere else, literally moving it on. But the refugee crisis was not going away.

Citizens across Europe were thrown headlong into a crisis that emerged suddenly from nowhere and raised lots of angry questions: Who is responsible? Who needs to take charge, to lead? What is the solution? (And importantly) Where did it start?

Five years earlier, in December 2010, a Tunisian fruit vendor, Tarek el-Tayeb Mohamed Bouazizi, had set himself on fire and died. It was a desperate act. In a note he left behind, he said that it was a protest in response to harassment and the confiscation of his wares by a municipal official and her aides. His despairing action became a catalyst for protests and political change in Tunisia that escalated into protests and violence across North Africa and the Middle East, reaching Syria—over 2,000 miles away from Tunisia—where challenges to the established regime resulted in civil war. With the resulting displacement of an estimated 11 million people, 5 million left the country as refugees.

This example illustrates the challenges leaders face in an interconnected world: Our action in one part of the globe—in this case Tunisia—can unlock a flow of consequences that ripple outward over thousands of miles, affecting millions of people. For those living in a border town in Hungary the problem they are facing—the influx of refugees—arrives inexplicably from beyond their horizon. Any solution they attempt will at best be temporary. The Syrian refugees are just as powerless, at the mercy of forces over which they have no influence. Their immediate problem— to find refuge and safety—is denied when they are simply moved along.

Similarly, as a leader of an organization, whether you are operating in a single country or across many countries, if you don't know exactly what is the root cause of the problem that your organization is facing, how can you work out a solution? Think of the banking crisis of 2008 and its impact. Think of Brexit. Too big, too complex you might say. Yet such is the operating reality in the 21st century for the leaders of organizations big and small. We operate in such a complex world, with so many linked and moving parts that the cause of our problems is often distant from us, and the wider effects of our actions (including the unintended consequences) can neither be anticipated nor seen. Those we seek to influence are grappling with other pressing events that we don't know about. We and the other players in this game are operating blind, interfering with and blocking one another's moves. When events spiral out of control, it becomes urgent to scale up our response, making it necessary to reflect on how we are operating as leaders.

To add to the leader's woes, this increasingly complex world is moving at a faster and faster pace. Our connectedness over greater distances creates the impression of time being compressed, so that we are forced to take action ever more quickly. Compare this with the luxury of the late 20th century, when a written response might take 2 or 3 days to arrive, giving you the time to reflect and consider before acting. Today, with a whole range of instant messaging tools at our disposal, the lack of an instant response shows indecisiveness or inefficiency. It can feel as though any response will do as long as it is quick and gets the problem off your desk, like a game of *pass-the-parcel.*

Alongside the added complexity and pace, the incredible amount of information at a leader's fingertips via the Internet is a treasure trove that our predecessors could only dream of. Leaders can analyze ad infinitum, as if peeling off layers of a giant onion only to find more. We risk becoming buried under information, unable to make a decision. How often have you said, But we need more data; let's just do a bit more research; we'll get the consultants to complete the analysis. How does a leader know when enough is enough?

Taken together—connectedness, scale, speed, and information—can leave us feeling overwhelmed as leaders. This effect runs across our teams and ultimately to the entire organization. What can we do in the face of this challenge? How should we equip everyone to survive?

One defensive response is for the leader to place the responsibility for solving a complex organizational problem in the hands of a single person, or a few designated people, relying on their authority and the usual hierarchy. Helpfully, this limits the number of perspectives and voices, producing a sense of certainty and clarity. The challenges no longer seem so complex after all. But this simplifying response does everyone a disservice. It is only a comfort blanket for those you lead who crave the strong, single voice.

A leader's second defense is to focus on projects to adjust the organizational structures, culture, and process. But this brings everyone's eyes off the ball to focus internally instead on defending what you have. It might work in the short term, for the larger organizations with the muscle to withstand external shocks. But it is not a strategy for long-term success because you are leaving new opportunities every day to be grabbed by more nimble competitors, while new challenges requiring immediate responses arrive unnoticed. Your organization moves unerringly toward irrelevance.

The third defensive response for a leader faced with organizational uncertainty is to create committees and working groups without authority. These can insulate you from accountability and defer decision making. The buck never stops with you, as long as you constantly surround yourself with a blur of urgent busyness.

Those three defensive strategies are flawed because the leader only creates the illusion of control, while failing to deliver a timely or an adequate response.

So what can we do instead for our organizations to thrive? We believe that the job of the leader, the team, and the organization is to position themselves to respond to the one certainty: The world is going to change, and quickly, and probably unexpectedly. The answer we will describe is to create conditions in which everyone can get smarter and faster. We want to create conditions in which the organization uses its collective wisdom to learn and adapt, and at speed. This approach has resilience at its core.

We call it *dispersed* or *distributed* leadership. By *leadership* we mean any activity that influences the motivation, knowledge, or practice of other organizational members (Spillane, 2006). The proposition is that, since we want to increase the speed and intelligence of our organization's response to change, we need our people to share what they know, to integrate it quickly with what others know, and to take decisions on the basis of that information. Just because they have a particular title, no one is written into or out of a leadership clique. While there are formal positions in the organizational hierarchy, *dispersed leadership* allows the role of a leader or follower to be dynamic, because the organization's best response arises when no one is rigid or impervious to the information and influences that arrive from partners, customers, suppliers, and colleagues, outside the hierarchy of our own line management. We use the term *leader* for anyone who influences other organizational members, earning that label in the moment by undertaking the leadership activity itself. We can be followers in one moment or situation and leaders in the next. This is real life. We are constantly influencing one another, making the choice to be adaptable leaders who are at the same time followers listening to and influenced by all the leader–followers surrounding us.

But how do we do this? How do we create the adaptable organization thriving in the face of an uncertain and rapidly changing world? The answer might appear simple: Leaders create leaders.

It's a clear proposition and here we are giving you the story of how we came to it. The story includes real up and downs, successes and failures—and we will share what we learned from that journey. It is a story about sparking the motivation in others to be leaders, and it is about you finding your true work as a leader. At its heart is a kind of leadership shift that must happen in all our organizations and society at large, if we are to find the courage not only to survive the most difficult and frightening challenges facing us today, but also to contribute to making things better. Read on . . .

CHAPTER 2

Preparing for Change

When Tony and Philip first met some years ago in a wet and rainy London, Philip's organization had just embarked on a new global strategy. This was long before the credit crunch and the refugee crisis in Europe. Philip's executive board had given him the difficult task of leading a merger of the East and West Africa business units to form a new integrated region. It was quite a tall order because these very disparate regions were delivering poor performance and operating largely in isolation from each other and from the wider organization.

As one of the board's newly appointed regional directors, Philip was left in no doubt about the urgency or the scale of transformation required. He wanted to move quickly in merging his East and West Africa teams, to get them operational as soon as possible. To do that, he needed a business vision and a plan for delivering it. He wanted the new region to be at the forefront of the wave of change rolling across the global organization; otherwise, he feared, they could all too easily become victims of it.

So newly promoted, bright eyed, and eager to move at once, Philip decided to call his new senior managers together. But he wasn't naïve about what he was taking on. He would be working with a wide range of experienced executives who between them had seen it all. Everyone regarded this territory as a no-hoper, languishing at the bottom of the company league tables. No one expected investment here to deliver big results, and it was expensive to operate in such a volatile environment, so they lived with the constant demoralizing threat of cuts. Might there be resistance to change?

How would Philip's arrival be greeted? Would colleagues feel resentful toward a younger and less experienced peer promoted over them, and would his West African colleagues be suspicious toward one previously based in East Africa? There would be multiple agendas in the room. How could Philip possibly see all these agendas? How would he bring these into the open? How could he bring people to engage with each other? How would he achieve alignment and build a team?

Philip wanted a facilitator to share the heat, and a colleague who had read Tony's book, *Diary of a Change Agent,* suggested Tony. Philip was drawn to the reflective approach described in the book, which chimed with his own belief that the immediate business gains you can achieve after mergers or change will only be sustained if at the same time you work toward long-term culture change. Tony brought Ben Parker, a colleague from his consultancy network, to the meeting. They struck Philip as a good combination: Tony using questions to draw Philip out and coaching to explore and grip the issues, while Ben was being the *hard man,* more in the face, trying to clear a path through the jungle. For Tony, the project in Africa contained the familiar challenges of leadership and engagement during any complex program of change, but brought these into a totally unfamiliar and multicultural context. While excited by this, Tony was also wary not to get blinded by Philip's obvious enthusiasm. He asked Philip what outcomes were needed and Philip almost too quickly replied, "At the end of three days, I want a shared vision and an agreed transition plan."

When Tony pushed him to articulate what he intended to happen longer term, Philip replied, "I've learned that real success only arrives if you can push leadership down so that people take responsibility, joining up in teams to address their common problems, and what I really want is to release the creativity and intelligence of all 500 people in my business."

It was unusual for Tony to meet a leader so confident in the potential of other people. Philip's words carried experience and humility, and made a lot of sense: Here was a real chance, and a rare one, to build a high-performance organization, and this ignited Tony's enthusiasm. Suddenly he felt willing to invest the energy to take on the challenge.

They explored Philip's vision further and it became plain how ambitious it was. The current reality was 500 people physically divided across 11 different countries, split between East and West Africa. Typically working in isolated offices of around 40 staff, people knew and cared very little about the merger. Mostly African, the majority of staff were doing routine, relatively low-paid jobs, with their instructions passed down through a hierarchical chain of command from an expatriate UK country director. Each country had a different culture, with a particular blend of ethnic, tribal, and religious influences, but most shared a colonial legacy that still affected the feelings and behavior of staff. Philip noticed a *feed me* attitude, even among quite senior people: Staff failed to deliver on promises, avoided responsibility, and passed problems back up the line. Philip wanted a high-performance culture and believed that this required a fundamental transformation of attitudes and behavior. When Tony asked how he intended to release the intelligence of 500 staff, Philip just said, "We will begin by bringing together 30 leaders."

At the start, we did not know how the 30 leaders would carry forward the merger with the wider staff of 500; we were simply seeking to create an aligned leadership community. Philip's initial questions about engaging the leadership community were as follows:

- Who are the most important people to have in the initial group of 30?
- How do I bring the opportunity to them?
- How much thinking and planning do we do before it is time to get on with it?
- How do we balance the need to deliver results with the need to change?

Tony and Ben, both experienced members of a consulting network that assists executive boards and leadership teams to engage people during business-driven change, shared with Philip their knowledge of three agendas originally set out over 2,000 years ago by Aristotle and that leaders need to embrace (Marlier and Parker, 2009):

- The strategic *thinking* agenda
- The behavioral *doing* agenda
- The engagement *feeling* agenda

Typically, the leader begins in blind enthusiasm, thinking like a finance or logistics director: What is the business case? What are the logics, benefits, and costs? What are the big tasks and when do we need to do them by? What level of performance do we need to attain? It is quite right that leaders address the *thinking agenda* because it is their job to set out the rationale and a pathway for moving forward. However, this tends to unleash a tsunami of activity, called the *doing agenda*, in an urgent effort to operationalize the change. Suddenly there are pressing demands on each person in the organization to produce plans, objectives, budgets, campaigns, logo, signage, systems, structures, job descriptions, responsibilities, resourcing, skills, rewards, incentives, and management processes. Phew! With this swirl of internal activity, it is not surprising that corporate performance and motivation take a hit. What the leader is in danger of missing is their key role in transforming the emotions of their team.

A leader attuned to the *feeling agenda* slows down and becomes emotionally intelligent. They remember how change can damage a person's ego, identity, and life-support system. They include the *logic of emotion* and pay attention to what people are feeling. They contain the fear while tapping into courage, passion, creativity, and positive excitement.

How do they do this? The leader is the first one to change their behavior. The leader inspires people with a relevant story. The leader shares vital information about why change is happening, often with an uncomfortable dose of reality. The leader challenges them to digest the new reality and gives support to bring out the choices ahead. The leader asks a few sensible questions, then shuts up and listens to the words and feelings coming back. When the leader pushes problem solving down to their followers and steps back to enable them to fill the leadership space, this sends a powerful message.

All three of us came out of that London meeting energized and with the courage to embark together on something quite challenging that we had never tackled before. Our collective willingness to take on this challenge grew out of the moment when something clicked for Tony after Philip expressed his ambition. Our collective capacity was made up of the different resources, experience, tools, and ideas we each recognized in the others. Our collective confidence was bolstered by a learning agreement we made: We would conduct regular and frequent reviews, sharing successes, learning lessons, and adjusting our roles and priorities as necessary.

Looking back, these three principles of *willingness, capacity,* and *confidence* allowed us to step together into the unknown and became key to delivering a successful change journey. This applied not just to the three of us as leader and facilitators, but also to everyone who became involved.

Three years later, something surprising was happening. Solid evidence of positive business results (numbers of customers, levels of income and costs) was beginning to pile up; staff morale was rising and staff confidence in the region's leadership hit a staggering 74 percent (measured by Ipsos MORI), beating the best public and private sector organizations in the United Kingdom. Against the expectations of people inside and outside the no-hoper East and West Africa Region, the merger was a success.

That was when people in headquarters began asking why this was happening. At first we found it hard to explain, until we hit upon the idea of an illustrative fable. It began like this:

Fable of the people who turned into hippos, lions, and gazelles

The people in the villages worked hard, and the rains watered their crops. They were well fed and prosperous but sleepy with their success.

One year when the rains failed and the crops did not grow tall, the people carried on as before, saying, "We have stored enough grain." The following year the same thing happened, and the stocks became low. "Things will soon return to normal," they said, "Just you wait and see."

The villages in the East were different from those in the West with their own customs and ways of seeing the world. Each side assumed that they had little in common, saying, "We are all like this but they are all like that." Both claimed their warriors were tougher and their wines tastier. There had never been a compelling need to find out what they had in common because a great desert separated them and their people rarely met.

In fact, East and West were less different than they thought. Each included diverse people from many tribes and traditions: some friendly others formal, some quiet others pushy, some compliant others dominant, and so on. And since they hardly recognized their problem with the rains, they had no desire to seek help from the other side.

As the fable continued to its conclusion, people became interested and said, "Yes, that's a real campfire story. But what is it really telling us?" We said, "It is telling you as a leader what you can do to deliver sustainable business results and ensure your merger or change program will succeed in the longer term."

Here we will give you the full story of what it takes to align 500 people in delivering organizational change. In this case the leader had to produce a fundamental shift in delivery. Hundreds of well-loved local products had to be killed off, in favor of a handful of big, cross-regional blockbusters. Offices had to close. New teams and reporting lines had to be created affecting 500 staff.

We will tell the story in five phases: Each time the leadership team, but with several members changed, gathers in a different African city, then disperses a few days later in airplanes to their home countries. Many months pass before they come back together, and on arrival everyone needs to retell the story so far to pick up the threads. Writing this story was like pushing a pause button on the change process: Helpfully the timescale was stretched, because of the distance and the infrequency of meetings, to reveal a to-and-fro of influences between leader and team and how this was harnessed to tackle the cultural legacy of dominance and subservience. With these difficulties amplified, you will find captured here a story of change, containing both the essential details and the rich complexity.

We now realize that the five phases contain key shifts in leadership emphasis that will drive engagement and deliver high performance, but not only in Philip's organization. The diagram we produced (Figure 2.1) describes the pathway any leader can follow to disperse their leadership and enable their organization to thrive.

There are many voices in the story: Philip's, Tony's, and those of several participants in the change program. In each of the five phases, we give you a similar, recognizable structure. One of us—Philip or Tony— begins with *the challenge* that is key to that phase, then tells *our story* supported by the voices of some of the team members who participated. The remaining sections of each chapter are from both the authors, except where we specifically indicate Philip's or Tony's voice. Under *How do you approach this phase?* we offer the key theories, principles, and ideas that

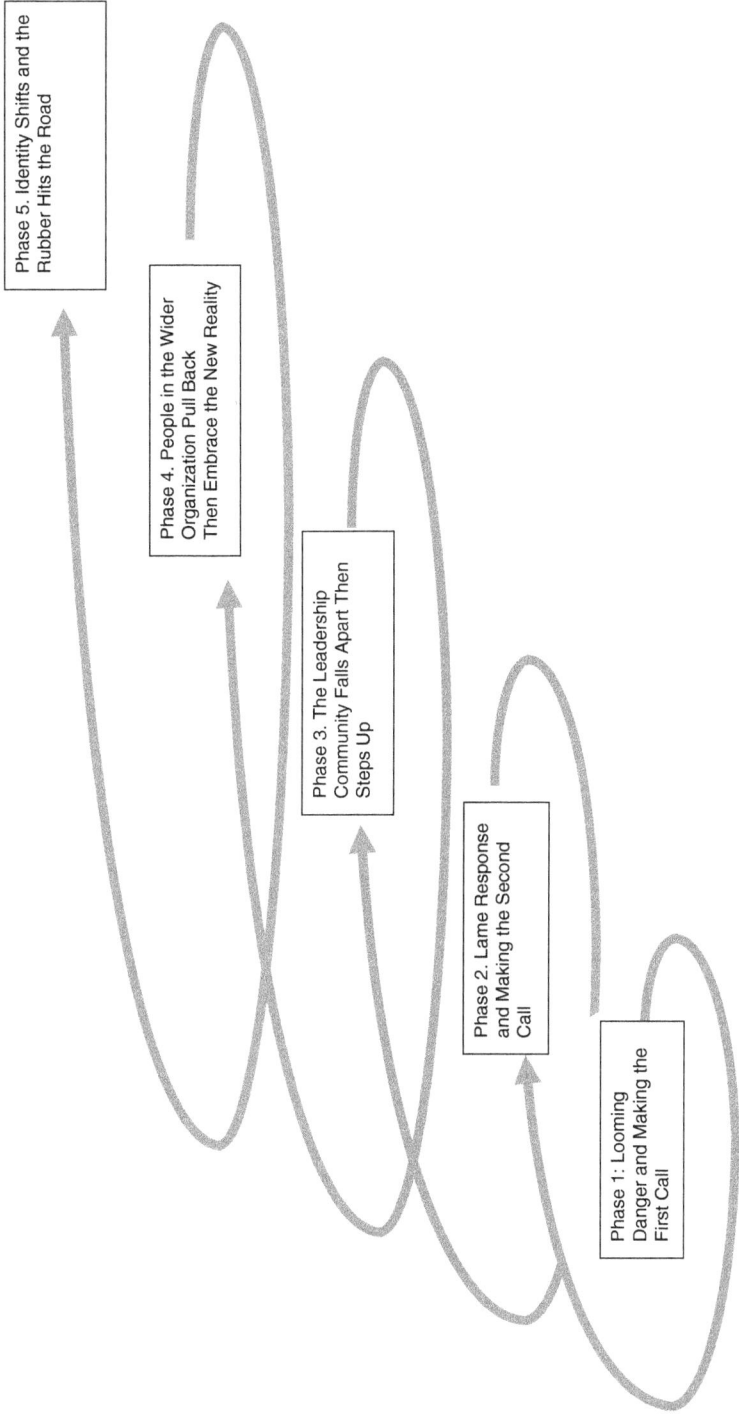

Phase 5. Identity Shifts and the Rubber Hits the Road

Phase 4. People in the Wider Organization Pull Back Then Embrace the New Reality

Phase 3. The Leadership Community Falls Apart Then Steps Up

Phase 2. Lame Response and Making the Second Call

Phase 1: Looming Danger and Making the First Call

Figure 2.1 The five phases in our story

13

underpinned our approach, to help you understand the *signs of progress* that follow. We then give you the *tools* that we used and *evidence of completing this phase*. Each chapter ends with a visual aide-mémoire and some *tips* to support your work as a leader.

In the final chapter we express the principles we learned from this experience, for you to follow if you want to become a leader who creates leaders.

PART 2

The Story

Hippos roaring at each other, gazelles isolated

CHAPTER 3

First Phase: Looming Danger and Making the First Call

The Fable (*continued*)

The sleepy people were blind to the looming danger that a brave young chief saw clearly. The first thing the young chief did was to call all the chiefs from East and West together. He told them, "The rains are changing. We must combine the skills and resources of East and West and face this together. If we do not adapt, we are storing up great problems for ourselves that may threaten our very existence."

But the chiefs did not believe him. Unafraid and fierce like a lion, the young chief waved his stick at them but like old male hippos—big, thick skinned, and sedentary—the other chiefs were hard to rouse. The young chief didn't give up. He continued to provoke and prod the old chiefs. Then, irritated and tired of the young chief, and slightly in fear of him, the other chiefs suddenly turned on one another, not just East against West but indiscriminately, and the young chief looked on with disbelief.

Finally, after much bellowing and baring of teeth, a single plan was agreed and the young chief went away exhausted, believing he had settled the matter and had called the chiefs to action.

The Challenge

You know what has to be done and there's no time to be wasted. You bring people together and tell them "This is important. We're under threat and we've got to move quickly if we're going to survive," but the tragedy is they don't get it. It's as if you are in a dream. The building is on fire but no one gives a damn. You're shouting, "Move, move, get out . . ." but no one hears you. Or they hear you, stand up slowly and just sit down again.

Philip: Our Story

It's a beautiful day outside in Nairobi. The sun is shining on the lake in front of the hotel. Behind the lake, some tourists are finishing a round of golf. There's a soft breeze blowing through the open windows of our meeting room. It's the sort of day when you feel content with life. My East and West Africa leadership team has come together in Kenya, which has long been a tourist destination for Europeans and North Americans keen to experience its wonderful combination of beautiful and varied landscapes, abundant wildlife, and superb beaches gazing out on to the Indian Ocean. The service culture here in hotels and restaurants is excellent: Not only do they defy Western perceptions of how Africa *can* deliver, they also defy other Africans' expectations.

The group listens politely as I'm speaking. The coffee break is due in an hour and my team members settle deeper into their chairs. Why worry when it's clear just by looking outside that all is well with the world?

But here I am explaining the challenges facing our organization, trying to paint as vivid a picture as I can, trying to make it real, simple, and inspiring! I have the task of leading the merger between the East and West Africa operations. This is a promotion for me. It's my first strategic leadership role and I'm meeting my new team for the first time all in one room. I'm a little nervous and I've been up early, practicing what I want to say.

I've got to deliver a significant change program and there's some urgency to getting this done. Yes, Tony and Ben have made me aware of the different agendas (thinking, doing, feeling) that an effective leader has to address with their team, and I have the intention of addressing this. But the truth is I'm predominantly in *doing* or troubleshooter mode, impatient and ready to push people hard to make the change. What needs to be done is clear to me and I anxiously want to galvanize people into action. With hindsight it's perhaps a little too early to be like this when I haven't even yet met everyone!

I knew I would face a big challenge around the culture of this team. Historically, the management style had been somewhat hierarchical and paternalistic. This was a legacy of the African colonial past but also of a historical tendency toward a bureaucratic and civil service style within the organization in which individual responsibility and initiative were limited because management *looks after* the team. Ian, a UK-appointed country director from West Africa, reflected how he and his colleagues were not particularly eager to change:

> There was a kind of lateral grumbling with colleagues. It was quite difficult to envisage what the benefits would be . . . it seemed local autonomy was being taken away, and to put it crudely, money would be taken away from us and allocated to regional activity that would be kind of homogenized and not entirely relevant to us here.

In calling the group together, my first step was to widen the pool of people that make up my new leadership team. Ten out of eleven of the heads of country operations in my team were from the United Kingdom, and nine of them were men. To get a wider set of champions for change across the organization, I invited 11 African senior managers—one from each of the business units—to join the leadership group. This was a first: The leadership team was now half from the United Kingdom and half from Africa, and a third of the leadership positions were taken by women.

For me, this was a watershed moment, a screaming headline of intent. It's as though I have been sitting round a campfire in the warmth trying to tell a story but outside the circle there were people I couldn't even see in the darkness but I knew they were there. I ask the circle to widen and invite those unseen faces to come nearer, to get warm and to hear what I have to say. I wanted to draw more people close to me as a leader. I wanted to send a clear message:

> We need wider involvement in strategic decision making down the organization. We need African voice in this team and I want to hear and respond to that voice.

This seemed to strike a chord with the African team members right from the start, although Binte from Senegal in West Africa was not expecting it:

> When I was asked to attend that workshop it was a shock and I wondered why me but I took the challenge because, in the

past, it was like I was in the shadows but being called into the leadership team, I was into the merger throughout and because of that I didn't find it a problem.

Fatima from Sudan in North Africa was uneasy, but at the same time, eager to see what change would bring:

I was nervous because we didn't know what regionalization would mean for us. West Africa was definitely a stranger but I was also excited because to me it would bring new opportunities, new faces, and new things to learn.

Otim from Kenya in East Africa could already see practical benefits to the organization from widening the circle:

Having African senior managers in the group meant that we demystified the leadership team meeting because for staff back in country it was much harder to believe UK country directors. Some staff are suspicious of UK management, and say, "Yes, right! Like you tell us everything!" But if the messages come from an African senior manager, well that helped improve things. It meant a lot more dialogue so everyone knew what was going on.

But Otim was not yet convinced about the plans to regionalize:

There was talk about people being given power or more control at the regional level as opposed to in the United Kingdom. There were all these things going through my head but I wasn't too sure. There was a bit of "Yes we need decisions to be made faster" but also "Will this really happen?"

As this new group arrived in Nairobi, I enjoyed my first experience of bringing together people from across Africa. Strangely, it is often easier for African professionals to travel to Europe or to North America than to other African countries particularly across the East–West African route. Many of our African team members had never travelled to each other's countries before, and there was a real delight in discovering new things about their continent and meeting fellow Africans in their home countries.

The question we set out to answer at this meeting: How will this merger produce synergies—greater impact and relevance at lower cost? We had a 3-day program of intensive work to answer this. The venue is great, the mood is good, but our luck doesn't hold: Ben goes down with flu and can hardly stand. We're already one man down before we've started!

As the meeting begins, I quickly pick up an underlying cynicism from the group as though they are thinking: "Leaders come and go, as will their ideas. What makes this new guy any different? We'll simply ride this one out."

In this comfortable environment, without the pressures of the day job, you can almost hear individuals thinking: "What really matters is not these abstract corporate concerns but what I'm doing in my country operation. We'll do a bit of talking here and then I'll go back and get on with the real work."

As Ian, one of the country directors, said, "If I'm honest, looking back we shrugged our shoulders and said we'd get on with what we were already doing."

Tony, Ben, and I guessed right that most of the senior managers present—let alone the other 470 people who worked in the organization across East and West Africa—knew and cared very little about the new region *or* the new corporate strategy *or* the coming financial squeeze *or* the changing context that was giving rise to it. As Akello from a provincial office in Sierra Leone said,

> I was saying to myself "is the organization really serious or are they just going with the fads . . . there's probably all new management and they want to show off that they've come up with another beautiful idea!"

As the 3 days progressed, we moved through a process of setting out the challenge, getting to know who we were in the room and where we were as a team, before starting to set out a transition plan that would help us move from where we were now to meeting the new challenges.

The initial sense of pleasure and excitement soon turned to struggle. Yahya, a senior manager from Ghana in West Africa, noticed how people had different perspectives on the merger:

> It was like the case of seven blind men touching an elephant and describing the elephant by the parts that they touch.

Time kept running out because people were unable to let go of their concerns and wanted to return again and again to the issues. We asked the group to prioritize the challenges facing us and when the exercise was almost complete someone piped up, "But what about issue number 17? Isn't that important?" and the group started again, dancing round the issue, exhausting each other but not moving forward. As Tony observed,

> This group could literally talk for Britain! And they hated decisions! They say they are "inclusive" but they're poor at listening, stifling others—particularly subordinates—and they can be brutal in doing so, railroading those who don't agree with them.

Ultimately, no one wanted a final decision about anything because that would mean letting go.

At the start of the meeting the new African members of the leadership team had been positively surprised: "This is a workshop that is dealing with real issues of strategic importance and you want our input!"

But after several sessions when the UK heads of operation still dominated and were in many respects, territorial, like hippos fighting—everyone else gets out of the way—the pressure was building up. On the final day a dramatic moment arrived when Fatima had had enough:

> I actually stood and said, "I feel we, the local members of staff, are not participating fully and I don't see the point of attending if we are not given the opportunity to talk freely and to be heard." There was quite a big silence in the room!

This divided the group into those who under time pressure felt it important to push on and get a result and those who said it was important to pause and address Fatima's point. Facing this impasse, Tony and Ben instructed each table to conduct a review of how people felt about the progress we were making and how the behavior of group members was contributing or not to that progress. They were asked to listen briefly to each person in turn without responding (see *tools* later, *five-minute process review*) before continuing the work. This intervention recovered the meeting, allowing us to move forward.

In concrete terms, after much pushing, prodding, and coaxing along, we did finally produce a preliminary deal on funding the new region, a vision of what change would deliver for us, and a 12-month transition plan to deliver the merger as I had hoped. By the end, Fatima's smile had returned:

> This meeting really changed the vision I had of our organization. Before we used to receive emails about the strategy but going to this meeting, ideas were brainstormed and decisions were made about how we would be working in the future. It really opened my eyes!

Akello, who had been struggling to identify how working regionally could benefit her local office, had begun to find some answers:

> It was really beautiful to see everybody talking about what fears they had. It was a kind of a motivation for me that the concerns I had were shared by many other people and that we could overcome those fears by focusing on the same vision. Yes, it was really comforting and encouraging. But the concerns did not go away immediately. There was still that extra mile of deciding who were the people who were going to take this forward.

After the huge pressure to get a result many people clearly felt tired, rushed, and browbeaten. I had been huffing impatiently around the meeting and at the time I thought, 'Thank God! At least we've produced a plan. If we can go away and deliver this at least we'll be on our way!'

However, although the team *had* produced the transition plan themselves and *had* seemed to sign up to it, looking back there was a sense of "Heh, we've done our bit" and if you listened carefully, you could hear an underlying air of "We know we have to merge. Okay. But how, as far as possible, can we get through this without changing anything?" Looking back, Gabriel, a country director from Senegal, commented, "There was a core group that felt, 'You know we've been down this road before and we will adopt the same methods that we adopted then . . . and it will go away.'"

As we drove away from the meeting, I suddenly had this niggling doubt. Yes, we had the big plan but with all the pushing and shoving to come to a conclusion in the meeting, who now would actually take the actions? My fear was that it would just be me and a few immediate colleagues.

So did we really get these people leading the merger? No! Were we really waking them up? No! When I got back to my desk the next week, I couldn't forget the moment when one of our heads of operations had simply said, "I don't see what the big deal is here." It was clear that the team didn't yet appreciate the enormity of the change required.

How Do You Approach This Phase?

We all know that starting well is crucial. Linking back to the fable, Philip is in the leader attitude of the brave young chief who sees a looming danger and is unafraid to say so. He would naturally begin boldly like a lion but Tony and Ben were pointing out that, instead of scaring 30 people, if he would step back a bit, it might be easier to motivate others to think about the future and make a sensible plan.

Motivating People in a Very Challenging Task

In mergers, the people affected do not choose to merge, but one day they come into work and find out what is being arranged for them, a bit like a forced marriage. In this story, the decision to merge the African regions was taken by senior managers at headquarters in the United Kingdom. The managers in Africa had no choice. Research has shown that fewer than 20 percent of employees are prepared to make changes their leaders want them to make (Prochaska et al., 2001). But, if the conditions are right, a person can participate in changes imposed by others. So, under what conditions can people be persuaded to invest their energies?

It will be no surprise that a critical factor is helping people to find their motivation particularly when they are confronted by a very challenging task. We knew that Philip was expecting a lot from people. When you ask people to go on a long march, they are happier, suffer less stress, and perform better if you keep them fully informed about why they are marching, how far they have gone, and how far they still have to go. If the goal seems too difficult, they simply give up at the outset. People generally prefer to tackle a task in manageable chunks (Bresnitz, 1989). So, we began with a clear, doable objective for the meeting: to produce a transition plan. This was essentially a map that would help us find the answers to our challenge.

Framing the Challenge

How should you actually confront people with the issue? As leader, the ball was firmly in Philip's court: He had to *frame* the challenge for this group. Bill Torbert is a professor at the Carroll School of Management, Boston, with a worldwide reputation for improving the quality of leadership in firms such as Gillette, Price water house Coopers, and Volvo. He describes *framing* as the first of four speech acts that a leader needs to master to be influential and powerful in action:

> The leader too often assumes that others know and share the overall objective . . . Explicit framing is useful precisely because the assumption of a shared frame is frequently untrue. When people have to guess at the frame ("What's he getting at?") we frequently guess wrong and because the frame is veiled . . . we often impute negative, manipulative motives (Torbert, 2004, p 28).

By *framing* we mean explicitly positioning the work of the group: What is the purpose of us being here together? What is our shared intention? What are the dilemmas we face together and do we share assumptions about the situation and its challenges. In short, you put your perspective as well as your understanding of the others' perspectives out onto the table for examination.

Breaking the Ice

You need to quickly break the ice, building high levels of trust and confidence so that people willingly focus on the work to be done. Tony began by describing in a series of positive statements how people can work through change from feeling as though they are victims of that change to taking responsibility for moving it forward. He then invited people to tell each other about a time when they had successful experiences of working with someone from another country.

These techniques called *positive preface* and *success stories* are part of the method of *appreciative inquiry* developed by David Cooperrider (Cooperrider and Whitney, 2005) that builds trust quickly in any group, particularly where people do not know one another, where their cultures and backgrounds are diverse, or where there is suspicion. An example of a past success question is, "Tell me about a time when you were . . . ?" A future success question begins, "Imagine you fell asleep for two years and woke up to find that this team was producing an astonishing performance. What sort of things would you see happening?"

Getting Down to Work

As we found, it is particularly difficult to get a large group of people—who, like many senior managers, enjoy talking—to start thinking practically about the future and their role in it. Marvin Weisbord and Sandra Janoff (1995) have developed a large group engagement method called *future search*. This is extremely useful when people responsible for the future of an organization or community need to make a paradigm shift in their thinking and actions. Weisbord and Janoff's conclusion, from extensive worldwide experience of such conferences, is that if you want to get a group of people to think about the *future,* you first have to get them to think about the *past* and the *present.*

You divide the large group up into small, self-managing groups of eight seated on round tables and ask them to map personal, organizational, and global past events on a large wallchart called a *timeline,* which is then examined for patterns and insights. Weisbord and Janoff's key discovery was that if you ask participants to share their feelings, not just their thoughts, they tend to shift quite quickly from *moaning* to *owning,* and from *me* to *we.* They have experimented with different ways of preventing breast-beating and finger-pointing and come back to two questions: What are you proudest of? What are you sorriest about?

Conducting Effective Conversations

During the meeting, we observed a lot of negative comments in the form of harsh criticism, sarcasm, and cynicism and not a lot of encouragement, support, or appreciation in the conversations. How concerned should we be? Research undertaken by Marcial Losada (Losada and Heaphy, 2004) has shown that there are striking correlations between how people in a team interact with one another in business meetings and how their team performs. Losada and colleagues classified interactions in terms of positivity/negativity, inquiry/advocacy, and others/self. They found that high-performance teams displayed dramatically more positive comment (five times more positive than negative), slightly more exploration of others' positions (rather than just making statements of their own position), and an equal exploration of issues external and internal to the organization.

On this basis, we clearly had a long way to go!

What Are the Signs of Progress in This Phase?

1. When the leader has prepared by considering how to motivate, rather than just scare the group with the scale of the challenge (Prochaska/Breznitz).
2. When the organizational challenge is clearly and explicitly framed (Torbert).
3. When the ice has been broken, trust is growing, and participants are building confidence in their capacity to handle change (Cooperrider).

4. When the group is divided into smaller working groups that are letting go of the past, in preparation for thinking about the future (Weisbord and Janoff).

5. When the conversations are monitored for positivity, inquiry, and balance in order to identify the shifts in habits of talking that will accelerate individual adaptation and speed up decision making (Losada).

What Are the Tools You Can Use?

In this first phase, the leader can benefit from tools that provide collaborative ways to address certain key questions, including, How do you engage the leaders? Where are we now? What does the future look like? What are the first steps? Here are four tools that are useful in doing this.

No 1: Raising the Issues—Six Thinking Hats

When a group is not ready to talk about the future you can begin with a tool called Six Thinking Hats (De Bono, 2000). This is a structured brainstorm in which you gather thoughts about the company using each thinking hat in turn:

1. The facts (cool white hat)
2. The feelings (hot red hat)
3. The risks (gloomy black hat)
4. The opportunities (sunny yellow hat)
5. The really wild ideas (creative green hat)
6. The conclusions (sky blue hat)

We used this tool to help people identify the challenges and opportunities facing the merged region.

No 2: Visioning—5/1/3

There are better ways to envision the future than simple brainstorming. Visioning in its most powerful form opens different parts of the brain to those we generally rely on and creates memories of the future that are intentional pathways to focus and channel your energy.

Here are the steps:

1. Participants close their eyes and imagine waking up in 5 years' time, when the merger or forced change is complete and delivering real benefits to stakeholders, including staff.
2. You read out a simple script that walks them through a typical working day five years from now, asking them questions that cause them to notice many small but important changes in their workplace (What do you see, feel, hear, taste, and smell? What do you see when you look in the face of your customer or colleague? etc.).
3. Finally, lead participants back toward the present, pausing at a 12-month point in the future and a 3-month point to rearrange things in a way that makes the 5-year future possible.

When participants open their eyes they are asked to scribble down as much of their 5/1/3 vision as they can remember.

No 3: Transition Planning

When, after the imagining phase, you need to make change practical, this is how to develop a transition plan containing concrete next steps:

1. Pair people up to compare their visions, and then write Post-its capturing key points for display on wallcharts.
2. Small groups cluster the Post-its for each of the three future visions (5 years, 1 year, and 3 months) and produce a short sentence in the present tense describing what is happening.
3. Small groups present the sentences to the whole group. The facilitator asks for reactions, and about the links from one vision to the next.
4. Go to the 5-year vision and say, "If this is to be real, each cluster needs to become an area of work that is addressed now by this team."
5. Participants arrange themselves into workstream groups and decide the actions needed over the next 12 months. Their actions are posted

quarter by quarter on a large wallchart labeled *Transition Plan*. Plenary discuss and refine the plan.

No 4: Five-Minute Process Review

Transition planning isn't easy and subgroups can get stuck in disagreements or lose their energy. A problem in one group tends to spread and erodes the momentum of the large group. What can you do about this? You can use the five-minute process review as a fast, self-administered medicine:

1. The chair of each group suspends discussion of the topic, setting aside five minutes for a review.
2. The chair asks each person round the table very briefly to report on how they are feeling about the progress and behavior of group members while the others just listen without responding.
3. After all have spoken, the chair asks for any ideas about how to behave differently to perform better as a group.
4. The chair invites all to make the necessary adjustments to their own behavior.
5. Return to the topic.

What Is the Evidence of Completing This Phase?

- The leader may be tricked into believing others are engaged.
- Or the leader may feel frustrated or thwarted at the inability of the team to recognize or respond to the very real threat that they are facing. At this stage that is OK and normal!
- There has been some talking but no real doing yet. With the exception of a few individuals, the leadership community is largely standing back and united in trying to maintain the status quo.

The key aspects of Phase 1 are summarized in Figure 3.1.

Phase 1: Looming Danger and Making the First Call

Action: The leader alerts the leadership community to a threat to the organisation

Tools
- 6 Thinking Hats
- Visioning 5/1/3
- Transition Planning
- 5 Min Process Review

The challenge
For Leader: *How do I deliver this message?*

For Community: *How can I get through this without changing?*

Evidence of completion?
Leadership Community trying to maintain the status quo.

Leader thwarted or tricked into believing others are engaged.

Focus questions
Where are we now?
What does the future look like?
What are the first steps?

Sign of progress?
- Leader motivating not just scaring people
- Challenge is explicitly framed
- Ice is broken and trust is growing
- Small groups working from past to future
- Positive behavior in conversations

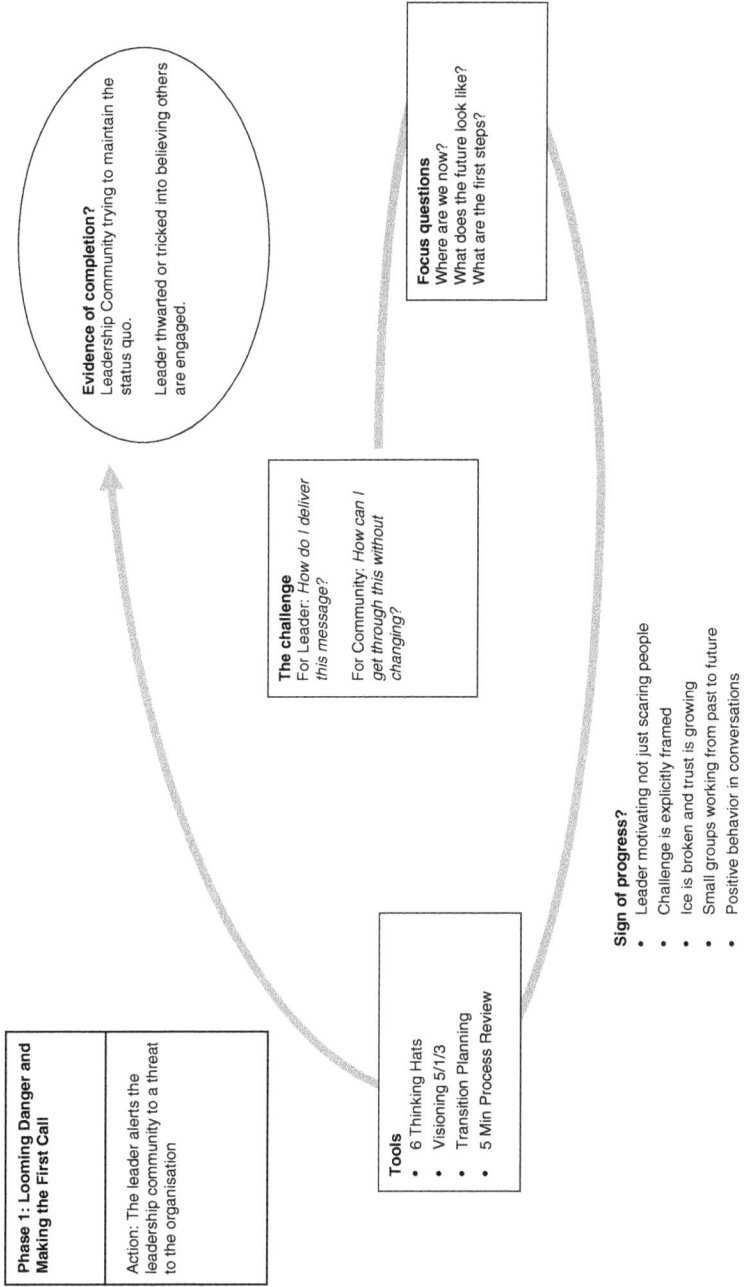

Figure 3.1 Phase 1 summary

Tips

- Don't let people drop in and out of your meeting. It is an organic process. To make sense of it and to build a sense of identity around the group, all of the team members need to be present full time in all the sessions. We have been to far too many meetings where people pop in, get only part of the picture, and end up disrupting the flow of discussions as a result and going away misinformed about where the team is. These people also disrupt the agreed actions at a later date.

- Spend plenty of time as a leader preparing the *framing* session. It is a critical step in getting the team to understand your motivation and intent as a leader. Allow lots of time for question and answer. This gives you a chance to demonstrate exactly what you know and what you don't. People will appreciate your honesty.

CHAPTER 4

Second Phase: A Lame Response and Making the Second Call

The Fable (*continued*)

The chiefs returned to their villages, but instead of doing what they had agreed, they said to their people, "Do not worry. Nothing has changed." Soon their people began to suffer: The rains were light again, food stocks were running out, and doubts grew within them.

When the young lion realized that the chiefs had failed to act, he became really angry. Waving his stick once more, he called on the chiefs a second time: "You have to accept that things have changed. We need to build a new future together and fast." He boldly took charge of the seed supply, sending more to the few chiefs who were adapting to suit the reduced pattern of rain.

At this, the simmering resentment of the hippos erupted. Some wanted to fight him for his high-handedness; others were afraid because he had shown his power, and one or two fell asleep because it was just too frightening.

The Challenge

It's as if you are in a dream with a crowd of starving people and there is a door with a big sign on it saying *Food*. You point to it but you're invisible. No one goes there. It's as if they want to continue suffering. You're desperate for a response. Do you shout louder, throw buckets of cold water over people, or shine bright lights in their eyes? What will make a difference?

Tony: Our Story

Arriving in an utterly unfamiliar and unpredictable place is how I experienced the second phase. Cameroon is one of the poorest countries on earth and puzzles economists because unlike Botswana, Chile, India, and countless other poor countries, it continues to get poorer. It is a nasty shock after the relative comfort and sophistication of Kenya, and on top of this, it is one of the rainiest places on earth. Through my taxi window I watched the baffling array of people on the muddy roadside: a skinny woman carefully roasting one tiny piece of sweet corn for sale, a couple of beaming lads balancing shoes on their heads as an eye-catching advertisement for the trainers in a big bag they dragged behind them, and a woman in a stunning bright purple and white printed wraparound dress, head erect and wrapped proudly in a matching fabric, tiptoeing between puddles.

Godlove, our taxi driver, demands an extra 12,000 francs "for gas" on top of our fare. We reluctantly agree. A few hundred meters later police stop the taxi to "fine" him for wrong registration plates, but Godlove expertly escapes their clutches. Repeatedly, the cab lurches alarmingly into fast oncoming traffic to avoid deep puddles, and then pulls up by a stall where Godlove butters up a plump, old machete-wielding woman. He moves two big bunches of bananas toward his car; then the woman objecting to the price Godlove offers waves her arms screaming, "Why you want to hurt me?" at which Godlove, feigning indifference, starts the engine as if to leave. This draws a weary nod of assent from the lady. Godlove pays, loads his bananas, and drives off laughing.

Drawing up to our hotel in Douala, Cameroon's second city, it is dark and we see scantily clad girls draped over the bonnets of bright yellow taxis parked on the hotel forecourt. The following morning drawn to my window by voices, I see a gang of men in matching yellow polo shirts and brown shorts jogging and chanting at the same time. I don't know what to make of it. It doesn't look like a sports team training. Could they be prisoners? A work gang off to a shift at the nearby docks? An army unit? I honestly had no idea. Perhaps I was in culture shock.

Those glimpses told me survival isn't easy here, and as I try to turn to the work in hand, I'm wondering: how would you really help someone in such circumstances? Is facilitation even useful or do people just need money? If the taxi driver had paid more for the bananas, or if we had bribed the police, what difference would this have made by tomorrow? Wouldn't the police just want more handouts? Something more is needed to change their fortunes—a different way of operating, a new mind-set.

Ben and I arrive to find Philip in full action mode: busy, impatient, and deeply frustrated. In spite of creating their vision and transition plan for the merger in Nairobi, in the ensuing months, his 30 leaders had done little. Their behavior seemed irrational because they were in real danger of losing income and having to close, not just a few product lines but whole offices, of having new systems and strategies imposed, of turning away loyal customers and losing capable staff. Why didn't they act to save themselves?

With a few close colleagues, Philip had taken charge of the sensitive question of which *core* products to continue and which *peripheral* products to kill, but he was caught now because he realized that he could not force product changes on the countries without turning his 500 staff into victims. Ian was one of this small brave group pushing the change forward:

> There were a number of influencers, Philip would have been one. And I was one of a group of people who were pushing the process forward. Putting it simply, with better projects operating in the country, better designed and reaching more people, our impact could be strengthened and our profile raised.

The reticence of the wider leadership team seemed to invite Philip to impose decisions but he knew this would be self-defeating both for them and ultimately for him. He must wake them up to the new realities if he was to harness their energy, knowledge, and experience to deliver effective and sustainable change. He wanted his staff to be leaders working together to transform their situation, but how were we to do this? This was the immediate question before us: How do we get the penny to drop so that 30 people in the leadership community really step up and take on a leadership role for the whole team of 500?

The meeting rooms of the hotel in Douala looked like sheds. There was wildlife from the pool area running through gaps under the doors. I saw a fat bright green lizard and Ben saw a rat. As the meeting assembled, I looked into the faces of 30 leaders and saw with horror how many had changed since Nairobi. I turned to Philip, who shrugged and said, "That's what we have to deal with." Country directors tend to take 3- to 4-year postings so he had lost a few and would continue to do so throughout this process. On top of this, he had sacked one country director for good reasons that he was not free to divulge to the rest of the group. Finally, many of the country directors had decided to bring different African senior managers from the last meeting so as to share the privilege of travel and expose more people to the leadership decisions.

Philip, Ben, and I had agreed on a shared approach to change based on *engagement,* which says that if you involve people in creating a collective goal, defining their roles, plans, and success measures, then they are more likely to perform because their work is meaningful and fulfilling rather than imposed drudgery. This was at the other end of the spectrum from a *bureaucratic approach*, which says that if a plan has been written up and made *official* then magically everyone will know it and work by it! But we needed the core leadership group to understand *engagement* if we were to make it work. Our advice to Philip was, in future, to ask country directors to bring the same African senior manager each time so as to stabilize this group.

Philip opened the meeting on an upbeat note, once again framing the challenges facing the region and the need to unlock the power of this group. After Nairobi, we agreed with Philip to work on inculcating the habits of high-performance teams and began a teamwork simulation to get people connecting and reflecting on their team behaviors. This addressed Philip's stated aim of using these meetings to build the capacity of the team to collectively respond to the challenges they faced not just in these meetings but in the months between. We described eight behaviors that help top teams perform (see *tools, holding up the mirror*) and gave out laminated cards for easy reference.

The team enjoyed the simulation, but only as an icebreaker, and overall they performed it badly. It was a struggle to get them to focus on how their behavior had contributed to their poor performance. They seemed happily distracted from the serious issues they were expected to be tackling. Nonetheless, table facilitators appointed from within the leadership team persisted and succeeded in getting the groups to make a contract to use the behaviors (active listening, questioning, summarizing, challenging, supporting, etc.) that would most quickly bring the real issues into the room.

The mood continued upbeat and in an aside, Ben whispered to me, "They're in denial." Yes, the jollity and false confidence exhibited by the team were clear signs that they were avoiding the threat they faced, but a review of progress on the merger brought a less frivolous tone. Although things were said to be moving fast, the individual country businesses were still not aligned to the regional and corporate priorities. The region was more a concept than a reality. Someone said that the merger was taking away their freedom, another that unless we can demonstrate relevance, we will lose key sources of income, and yet another, that trust is an issue across this team.

Then a great wave of excitement rippled round the room when we heard that London had won the 2012 Olympic bid. We continued the work and by the time we closed the first day the overall impression was of people starting to get past being polite and beginning to raise issues. That evening Philip reflected that the day's discussions had been "difficult". He referred to "unpleasantness" from one or two people. Ben added that one table had low energy. I remarked that some people were taking turns but holding back, while other noisy ones were dominating.

The second day started with the shocking news of bombs in London. Immediately this became a focus. We had to break for people to check on London-based friends and relatives, but on finding most of the phone lines jammed, we resumed in some uncertainty. As previously in Nairobi, we would find that the mood could turn suddenly and unpredictably nasty.

We brought in a group of external customers: young business people from the *outside world* who we thought could have a waking-up effect on the group, but there was little obvious impact. Then a headquarters visitor, struggling with our ground rule of "no PowerPoint," delivered the news that there was a massive restructuring under way in the United Kingdom and that HQ would begin to work radically differently. The immediate lack of response to one of the biggest headquarters changes in living memory seemed eerie but slowly, as we invited reactions, furrowed brows turned into angry questions that seemed to rail against the new era dawning:

> This is not the job I joined up to do. Are we just going to be reduced to administrators?
>
> Why are you pushing us— is the fast pace really necessary?
>
> Are you really asking us to discuss this or have you made all the decisions already?
>
> Is this the right way to go?

The anger showed that it was becoming harder for people to believe that they could continue the status quo but they were still holding tightly onto freedoms they had enjoyed for decades and onto a tacit understanding among them that someone, somewhere should continue to fund their diverse activities.

The big and difficult message was, "You will cease to exist if you do not deliver results," and this was bringing people back to uncomfortable questions such as, "What are we really here for?" And, "How do we get enough income to really make a difference?" Although the broad questions of purpose and impact had already been answered by headquarters in a 5-year strategy paper ("Our Impact to Reach Millions More People") this had not brought clarity to the minds of these 30 people or the 500 country-based staff, who each had a different way of describing what the company does. In this region, 500 staff were busy doing hundreds of commissioned projects and they were angry to be told that their work did not produce the needed impact. The threat that their projects would be stopped made them indignant, hurt, or insecure. Looking back, Akello from West Africa said she felt angry and she was asking herself, "What's wrong with what we are doing already? Isn't it enough, isn't it appreciated?"

Gail, a country director from Ethiopia, felt similarly:

> The anxiety was that there'd been all this stuff going on that was perfectly successful and why suddenly do we have to do something different.

Historically, 11 country offices with a public service mission, facing more than their fair share of the world's worst problems (poverty, conflict, insecurity, disease, lack of skills, lack of democracy, justice, corruption) had a queue of people knocking on their doors with worthy projects. Much of this work had been funded by the UK taxpayer. However, today, over two-thirds of the organization's funding is from new sources: fee-paying customers, a wide array of corporate clients, including many multinational corporations, and partners such as the European Union and the World Bank. This pulls the teams in various new directions, not necessarily toward the strategy. We could see people, deeply committed to their work, contemplating, grappling, trying to make sense of the change, weighing up options, and understandably finding it uncomfortable to let go. There was still a huge amount of anxiety in the group. As Binte from Senegal said,

> I had the fear of a cut in our budget and more being given to big-ger countries so that the amounts allocated for my country would be small . . . That's where the anxiety was. Initially, there were fears of maybe a reduction in the staff, of job losses, also of lack of capacity to deliver some of the products. Some staff felt "Oh this is like removing me from my own country setting and exposing me to a wider context . . . do I have the skills to fit the challenge?"

Ben and I took the loss of good humor, tunnel vision, and anger as signs of an old paradigm shaking and breaking apart, but for Philip the arrows pierced deeply. Outside during the break, he whispered earnestly to me about how members of the group were irritating him with their "feed me" attitudes. It seemed that he was getting caught in his own trap. He had been challenging people to speak out and now they were respond-ing honestly but he didn't like the negativity of their messages. He noticed "elephants in the room," including some fear and suspicion that arose from the sacking of a country director but his not being allowed to an-nounce why. We could see how one person had been speaking up in pro-test for another whose local office was closing. As people began to speak out, the exchanges had become increasingly unpleasant but some people were still "hiding under the blanket."

Philip's frustration came across as irrational, and a further sign of the shockwaves that ripple through everyone in a group, including the leader, when a significant mental block is shifting. I reminded him that earlier we had seen people polite, avoiding issues, distracted into digressions and departures, and lifted by denial into false jollity and that the anger coming up from the group was a positive sign of people starting to actively engage. I reassured him that the messages from customers and the United Kingdom underlined the legitimacy of changes he was leading. In other words, his team did not just see their regional director going mad, they could tell he was lined up with the United Kingdom and taking them in a direction they needed to go.

After the break, Philip pushed back with firmness bordering on anger, by confirming that future funding, instead of coming from the United Kingdom, would flow through his office and that countries needed to get used to new levels of accountability, with targets signed up to actually being met. Some uncomfortable facts about funding were put on the table: "Over 50 percent disappears into supporting our infrastructure," leaving another 50 percent that is frittered away on delivering countless small local products that are largely invisible and without measurable impact.

Unbelievably, I noticed someone asleep at the back of the room! Instead of leaders we still had a room full of victims: some complacent, others confused, shocked, or overwhelmed; some completely shutting down, and others exploding angrily as they found it increasingly difficult to remain in denial. The eight value-creating behaviors we had shown people the previous morning had been temporarily put to one side and people were disconnecting, sulking, or snarling at each other. Now the wave of emotion was affecting me too. Unusually, I was simmering with anger, finding it hard to focus and I could see that Ben was apoplectic!

Our dinner outing that evening was also a bit of a disaster. We climbed onto a private bus in time to reach a local riverside restaurant where at sunset you see the beautiful peak of Mount Cameroon reflected in the water. Somehow the driver misunderstood, got us lost and we missed the sunset.

When we arrived at the restaurant it was shut and they had no record of our booking. Finally, we persuaded the restaurant to open but it still took over an hour for food to come.

The third and final day we pushed the victims to shape up. I held up the mirror contrasting their behavior the previous day with that of high-performing teams. They struggled. One person complained of "jumps in the program," asking how today's work related to the previous day's discussions. During a report back from a subgroup, two people fell into an argument while others stood back and let them.

On a positive note, we were succeeding in getting more minority voices in the room, but usually in dissent. Philip, Ben, and I found that we could rely on the table facilitators to make constructive contributions and we did see a few other brave people step forward making quite impressive presentations but being denied the encouragement they deserved from colleagues. After we had painstakingly listed by name, hundreds of existing products covering all the customer-facing activities of all 11 country operations and clustered and sorted them into *core* (high impact, central to the mission of the organization—to continue) and *peripheral* (low impact, tangential to the mission of the organization—to be stopped), we gained agreement on the few big cross-regional products to take forward.

This left team members with some new dilemmas, asking, "Do I want to be part of this? Is this what I joined this organization to do? What is left of my role? Do I have a say or have all the decisions been taken?" They resented being asked to kill off hundreds of products they loved. For some, however, this was a turning point. As Akello said,

> I actually had a thought of moving on to do something else but then at the same time I felt one voice in me was telling me "no this is a new challenge, if you have the chance to do it, face this new challenge and it will probably teach me to do things differently."

Ian from West Africa, who had been more deeply involved in the work leading up to Douala, was more upbeat about the meeting:

> People did begin to see the benefits. In those months prior to this meeting, a number of barriers were broken, personal relationships were developing, and people were beginning to see action taking place. Obviously people have commitment to doing things and don't like the idea of stopping doing them but there was general recognition we were not getting far with our local products.

Most agreed that our 3 days together had been a long slog as we proved beyond doubt that an era was passing. Gabriel later observed the moment when change hits you emotionally:

> It was a real shock for me. After people understood the reasons for the change intellectually, it was only later that they really got what it meant for them personally and it was like a mini explosion!

Old ways of working were no longer possible, and people were not happy about it. At the end of the meeting there was a sad and defeated tone to people's closing comments. The *leaders* somehow felt abandoned. Philip acknowledged that he was asking a lot, recognized how difficult the meeting had been for everyone, and signaled that the teamwork they had started needed to be continued at a distance after everyone went home.

Ben and I went home cross but not surprised that the new people who had not had the benefit of Nairobi had failed to get it. An ambitious program, combined with unexpected events, had put the group into overload and they had reacted first by reaching for their phones, then by dipping in and out, and finally by appearing sad and confused, sensing trouble ahead. Although too much had been packed in, the end of workshop feedback was not bad, but we were not able to feel proud or professionally fulfilled by the outcome. We could not be confident that country directors would help their staff re-prioritize heavy workloads in order to make space for the new regional tasks.

How Do You Approach This Phase?

We tried to understand why this group had created and signed up to a transition plan in Nairobi but done little or nothing since. It seemed that, as in the fable, the chiefs had gone back home and told their people not to worry. As a result, nothing much was happening. Life in "the outlying villages" was continuing as usual.

Changing Attitudes and Behavior

"A leopard can't change its spots" is often said and usually with disappointment or bitter cynicism when an alcoholic, a gambler, a dieter, or an unfaithful partner lets us down by failing to change in the way that they promised and we hoped. We were disappointed but not yet in despair at the inaction since Nairobi, partly because of the wealth of evidence that proves change is possible.

For example Kurt Lewin, a pioneer in social psychology who escaped from Nazi Germany, demonstrated that for a group to perform intelligently it needs a particular kind of leader who is democratic not autocratic, and to bring about change the leader needs to "unfreeze" the group bringing an emotional stir-up to "break open the shell of complacency and self-righteousness." Lewin noted that a person's group is the "ground" for their perceptions, feelings, and actions, and the sum total of all motivations, conflicts, and forces in the group he called a "group field." So our job was to involve people, stir them up, and in the end transform the "group field" so that each person invests their own energy in making the merger a success (Lewin, 1997).

Leon Festinger, a social psychologist, followed Lewin with a theory of cognitive dissonance, in which he proposed that people experience psychological pain when their behavior does not match their attitudes (Festinger, 1957). For example, if a person believes that smoking is bad for them (their attitude), yet they continue smoking (their behavior), this creates a pressure that is likely to result either in a change to their attitude ("Smoking is not bad for everyone") or in their behavior (giving up smoking). If participants in our meeting wrongly believed that the work they had been doing in their countries was achieving the needed impact, Philip, the leader, could address either their attitudes or their behavior to bring about change. For example, he could address attitudes by presenting evidence that the work was not having the intended impact. At the same time, he could address behavior by getting people to try out something more effective like helping one another in bigger cross-regional project teams. Currently, people had neither the relevant information to challenge their attitude nor direct experience of alternative ways of working to challenge their behavior.

Letting Go of the Past

Since birth we have all been experiencing change in one form or another and it continues to our graves. We learn to change through participating in rites of passage such as 21st and 40th birthdays, moving homes and jobs, and weddings and funerals. But why is change sometimes so painful? John Bowlby (1951) described how small children attach themselves to their career, almost as ducks imprint on whoever is present at a critical moment. Later, without realizing, we become attached to our home, workplace, friends, workmates, even to our habits and ways of being in control. During change we must let go of the people and things we value, and this entails our identities and boundaries being fundamentally rearranged. We find ourselves painfully betwixt and between, being *lost* before being *found*. So how can we recover ourselves more quickly?

The early part of a merger or change program is often difficult and slow, in part because leaders, impatient for new beginnings, fail to honor the amount of time and support their staff need to make sense of what is happening, to let go of the past, and to move on. William Bridges (1980), building on earlier work by Elizabeth Kubler-Ross (1973) into bereavement, explained the difference between "change," which happens in the outer world, and "transition," which happens inside the skin and takes a little longer:

> (Leaders of change) . . . often forget that while the first task of Change Management is to understand the destination and how to get there, the first task of Transition Management is to convince people to leave home. You'll save yourself a lot of grief if you remember that (Bridges, 1980).

Bridges describes three phases in transition management: letting go, a neutral zone, and then, new beginnings. Letting go is the first priority and in doing so, the leader needs to clarify what is ending. In psychological terms, it is the opposite of a merger. It is a clean separation that requires a shared clarity of what is finishing and what isn't. It entails a celebration of success, an acknowledgment of the contribution from those in the team, and the leaving behind of emotional baggage such as blame, guilt, or sorrow.

Looking back with hindsight, we did not address letting go directly enough in Nairobi. Letting go is emotional and it is natural for people to be defensive, perhaps in fight, flight, or freeze, giving strong reactions. By the end of a Douala workshop that was deeply frustrating, most were grumpily realizing the inevitable but still isolated in grief for what they were losing.

Reading the Signs of Resistance

Without strong direction from us, the group would use up the entire meeting time talking without reaching any decisions. At the same time, Philip kept trying to push the group into action. We had been dragging the group to produce the transition plan while missing some of the signs of resistance from the group and in approaching the decisions to decommission some of the existing products, we noticed that the team was fearfully holding onto the status quo.

What were the subtle and easy to miss signs of resistance? William Schutz, a psychologist who helped the U.S. Navy overcome problems of conflict in submarine crews, identifies the following signs of resistance: holding rigidly to my position, not listening, misinterpreting, withholding, feeling misunderstood, being easily irritated or angered, avoiding certain topics, not wanting to probe, becoming confused, and losing my sense of humor (Schutz, 1994). He noticed that each of us has different defense mechanisms and identified six defensive postures people tend to take:

- Denier—there are no problems
- Victim—I am offended because other people are behaving aggressively/ unreasonably
- Critic—I know better than you and I pick up on everything that is not perfect, e.g., your grammar, your stupid remark, or your weak idea
- Self-blamer—everything that happens is my fault
- Helper—I look for someone to help whether they want it or not
- Demander—reassure me that I'm OK and there's nothing wrong with me

A psychologically healthy adult response to a changing environment is to be curious, self-aware, and discriminating—a person assimilates the information and resources that meet their true need. A leader has to extend an individual's awareness of their need and support them in making choices.

Working Through Resistance

When resistance is identified, then how do you best address it? Arnold Mindell's method is to recognize that each individual experiencing resistance needs to move through three different positions—as self, as other, and as fly on the wall—before they can resolve their inner conflict (Mindell, 1992). A facilitator's job is to help a person to express these positions through a process of reflecting on these questions:

- What is your point of view?
- What is your colleague's point of view?
- What do we each need now?

During this process people often make illogical and contradictory statements and can get quite emotional but the process itself allows a psychological shift to take place. Typically, not only does a person feel better afterward but they are then ready and motivated to take up their responsibility as a leader. Reflecting back on what she had learned from the process we went through, Foluke, one of the African senior managers, summarizes the approach we took like this:

I was resolved not to be deterred by resistance and not to ignore it either. But to understand it and so do something about it.

Creating a Sense of Urgency

John Kotter, a Harvard professor who studied 100 organizations (most of which failed in their efforts to transform), defines the first step of transformation as "creating a sense of urgency" that convinces at least 75 percent of the leadership community of the need for change (Kotter and Cohen, 2002). Typically, leaders are reluctant to give the negative information people need to persuade them that change is necessary. He went on to describe eight steps that need to be completed before an organization has completed a transformation:

1. Create a sense of urgency—we must do something
2. Build the guiding team—get the right people on board to drive the change

3. Get the vision right—give the guiding team a compelling vision to direct the effort

4. Communicate for buy-in—send credible messages and walk the talk

5. Empower action—remove barriers to people behaving differently

6. Create short-term wins—get fast results to diffuse cynicism

7. Don't let up—don't allow urgency to sag, create wave after wave of change

8. Make change stick—reshape culture, practices, norms, and values.

What Are the Signs of Progress in This Phase?

1. When team members are exposed to new points of view (as in customer research) and experiment with new behaviors (as in using new behavior in teams to bring the real issues out onto the table) (Festinger).

2. When team members are bitching and moaning, expressing a mixed up range of mostly negative emotions both about the past and the future, showing that they are beginning to detach and reevaluate the past; later, when this mood has passed they may be ready to celebrate the ending, clearly identifying what is over and what they are bringing from the past with them into the future (Bridges).

3. When the subtle signs of resistance are identified and people are challenged to get in touch with their true needs (Schutz).

4. When in spite of the corporate urgency, team members are given enough time, challenge, and support to fully contemplate and explore their dilemmas around what is changing, the benefits and costs of changing and not changing, and finding the real options and choices they have, leading them into a state of mind where they are prepared to change (Mindell).

5. When at least 75 percent of the leadership population are genuinely convinced that change is necessary (Kotter).

What Tools Can You Use?

In this second phase, the four tools that follow give the leader ways to engage others in addressing these key questions: What new realities do we need to wake up to? How do we get back in control? What can we keep? What do we need to let go of and how?

No 1: Direct Contact With Stakeholders Requiring Change

People need to know what is changing and to understand why. Rather than simply delivering secondhand wake-up calls through Philip or through emails from headquarters, we decided to bring specific people (customers from a new target group and a sponsor from headquarters) into the room to deliver *the need for change* message directly. This allowed Philip, as leader, to adopt a less adversarial and more facilitative position, helping participants grapple with the contradictions and making meaning out of it.

No 2: Three Circles

When participants are struggling with change and they feel like victims, we ask them in side conversations, what is in their three circles (Marlier and Parker, 2009):

1. The "outer circle" is sometimes called the "circle of doom" because it is the negative stuff that they cannot influence (see Covey, 1989, pp. 81–88). We offer them five minutes to "bitch and moan" about what is there, but then suggest they stop worrying and let go of concerns they can do nothing about.
2. We then ask them what is in their inner "circle of control," pointing out that for most people, even the richest and most powerful on earth, there are few things that they totally control without receiving permission from, or putting out their influence toward, others.
3. We ask them how they can extend their middle "circle of influence." Who do you need to connect with and influence and on which topics?

This is an approach that helps people recover a sense of capability and confidence. It recognizes that while our own knowledge and influence may be limited, by connecting with others we can unlock a collective wisdom and capacity. It opens up new possibilities for positive action, and typically, people report feeling better and more proactive after this exercise.

No 3: Holding Up the Mirror

For any team going through change, open, exploratory conversations are necessary. In the denial phase, as they face the harsh facts, buried issues and emotions need to be raised to the surface. In a team, this means each person needs to listen, question, and connect more effectively just when their defenses are causing them to fight, flee, or freeze. To achieve this, we show people how to see and speak about behavior. This gives them a greater sense of control even when they are experiencing some quite strong emotions in the letting go phase. So we conduct a short business simulation in which performance depends on information sharing and teamwork, and we teach people how to use eight value-building behaviors (active listening, open questions, summarizing, support, challenge, clarifying, timeout, and review) that give an edge to high-performance teams. We appoint and carefully brief table facilitators to work the value-building behaviors, reinforcing them through a behavioral contract and behavioral reviews. In each review, the facilitator holds up the mirror to show a group how they can adjust their behavior to raise their performance.

No 4: Managing Endings—Timeline

When a group is holding on to the past they become stuck, stressed, depressed, numb, or low in energy. You can use a tool called Timeline as follows:

1. Each person identifies their key events (good and bad) since joining the organization, writes them each on a separate post-it, and posts them on a chronological line on a long wallchart.
2. The group gathers round, asks questions, and looks for themes.
3. Each person then shares their proudest and sorriest moments and also declares something they needed to leave behind (a behavior or an attitude) and something they want to bring with them (a memento,

skill, or quality) into the future. As they take turns to make these declarations, they physically step over a line into the future.

What Is the Evidence of Completing This Phase?

- Ideally, all members of a team will have identified what to leave behind and what to bring with them. They will have drawn a line that marks the decision to change and stepped over the line from the past into the future.
- The leadership community may still feel sad, defeated, fragmented, and lost. It's an ending with a deep sense of loss and this opens the possibility of a proactive phase to come.
- Realistically, the leader and facilitators may be angry, having received the group's resistance.

The key aspects of Phase 2 are summarized in Figure 4.1 Tips

- Strike a balance between focusing on internal change and external delivery, and keep pushing for action.
- Don't worry when people express strong negative feelings—it can often mean that they are moving their attitudes and coming on board.

Seek facilitator/coach support to work through the negative emotion coming in your direction from others during the denial phase.

Phase 2. Lame Response and the Second Call

Action: The leadership community ignores the call and the leader pushes them harder.

Evidence of completion?
Leadership community stepped from the past into the future, but may feel sad and lost.

Leader may be angry, at the group's resistance.

The challenge
For Leader: *How do I wake them up?*

For Community: *Why is the leader being so stupid and nasty?*

Focus questions
What's new?
How do we recover control?
What do we keep?
What are we letting go?

Tools
- Stakeholder Contact
- Three Circles
- The Mirror
- Timeline

Sign of progress?
- People are being exposed to new attitudes and behaviors
- Resistance is recognized and explored
- The team identifies the dilemma, options, and choices they have
- 75% of the leadership community recognise change is necessary

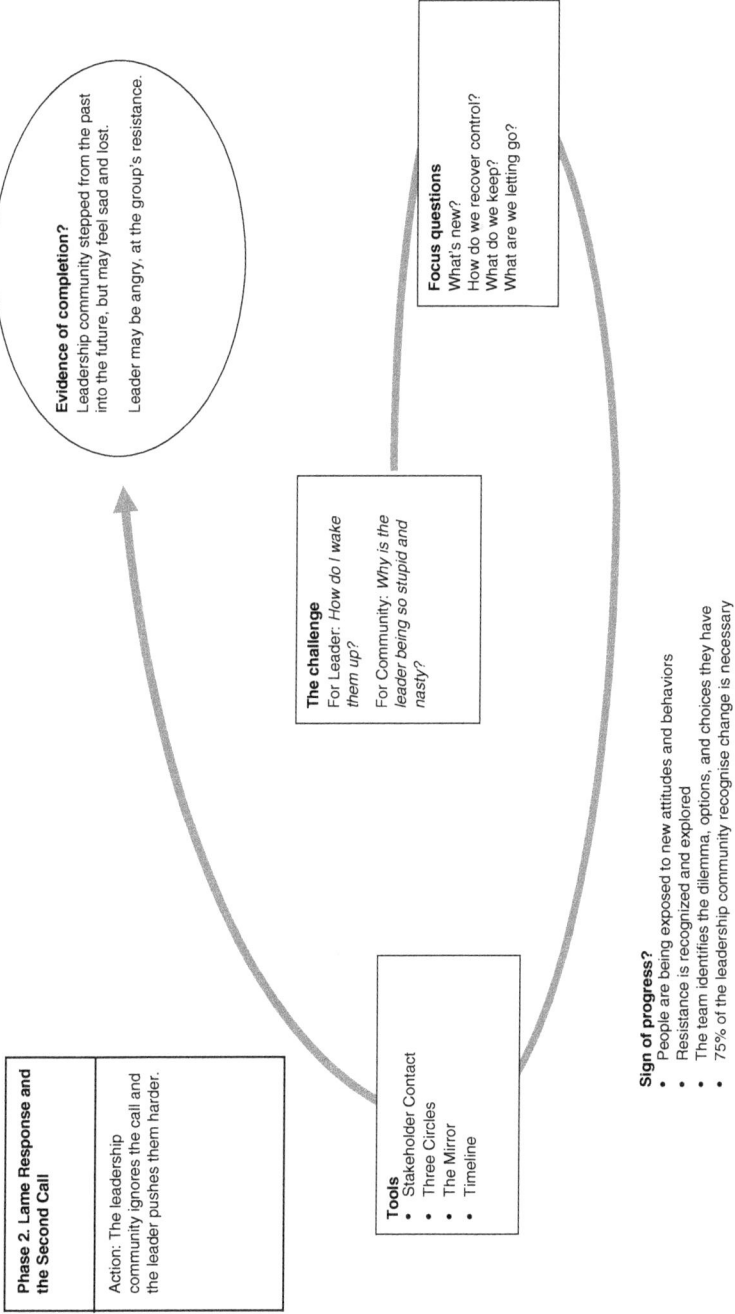

Figure 4.1 Phase 2 summary

CHAPTER 5

Third Phase: The Leadership Community Falls Apart Then Steps Up

The Fable (*continued*)

For months the hippos remained angry; some were confused. Then the mood turned to defeat as they felt the passing of a happy era. Starved of information, their people both in the East and the West felt more and more anxious.

Then happily one day the young chief discovered "a thing of beauty"—a new seed needing less rain, and despite his frustration, he gathered the chiefs a third time.

Remembering an old saying from his tribe, "One head does not contain all the wisdom," he decided there and then to change his approach. Instead of waving his stick, he simply pointed to the declining food stores and calmly stated, "There is no going back: Unless we accept this, we will all die." He asked the chiefs to sit together as their fathers and mothers had done in the old days, East alongside West, to decide on a solution.

They were gloomy but as the chiefs grappled with the challenge a new mood took hold, and they declared, "We have had a change of heart. We are all in the same boat and we need to work together!"

The Challenge

It seems that all we have achieved so far is to make people unhappy, confused, and scattered in all directions. How do we bring them together again and support them in becoming strong, confident individuals who, as part of a team, know how to change their fortunes?

Tony: Our Story

During the months following their cold shower in Douala, more of the leaders sensed the new opportunity in the air, including Gail from Ethiopia:

> People started challenging each other on why we were continuing to do some of the stuff that we'd been doing for years just because we'd always been doing it.

Already old certainties were breaking down and a new fluidity was being created in people's sense of who and what they were. Key individuals within the team—enthused through direct conversations and contact with Philip—were buying in to the change. As Gabriel from Senegal said,

> Philip is results focused, and is very energetic, supportive, and consistent in that support. His attitude is contagious—I caught that bug and went on to infuse the rest of the team.

There was more clarity among the team on the direction they were taking and the impact of not changing. Otim from Kenya noticed that Philip's leadership message, so often repeated, was slowly sinking in to work its magic:

> Personally, when you're moving me from one place to another, I need to understand why you're moving me so that I can help in the movement. So, to me, that clarity in the message was key.

If progress seemed slow it was not just that the leaders were being stubborn. The team was constantly changing as people were moving on to new posts elsewhere; their replacements arriving needed to figure out what to do and why. When Mark joined the region as a country director, he was confronted with a clear challenge:

> When I arrived here my line manager told me that this was the worst performing country in the region with people having worked here a long time becoming protective and silo-ed. So the first thing I had to do was restructure. It meant losing about half

the people we had. You do have to change the people—not all of them—to let go those who don't want to be part of it and nurture those who do.

Looking at the poor performance in the wider region, Mark was skeptical about whether and how it could be addressed:

Politically this region was a fairly low priority and had tiny amounts of money available. To put it bluntly, we were in bad shape, rudderless, and a bit self-indulgent and there were only two ways to go: further down, or up. My thought about the change was "here we go again" because we'd been shuffling this stuff around like packs of cards for the last decade.

Each member of the leadership team clearly needed a firm grasp of the issues, the strength of a supportive band of colleagues around them. Only with this could they prepare to make their best contribution during the journey their team was about to embark on.

In the wake of Tony Blair's Commission for Africa, the East and West Africa operation had secured new funding from headquarters to develop some big, new products. This was good news but it had the knock-on effect of complicating the annual budgeting exercise. Philip needed countries to understand the new arrangements and for country directors to sign up to the business they needed to deliver over the next 5 years.

By now, we were used to the group of 30 leaders talking endlessly and failing to reach agreement. So, with the team's next meeting in Addis Ababa fast approaching, we scheduled a full day at the start to thrash out how each country would contribute to delivering the regional targets. Determined not to run out of time, we were prepared to spend the whole 3-day meeting on this single issue if necessary.

Before the meeting, we asked ourselves how far we were in turning the 30 leaders into a team. They had left Douala with their heads down, apparently defeated and fragmented as if the former, superficial bonds that had held them together had been broken without any new bonds yet in place. In spite of this, Philip was getting a positive message from headquarters that the merger in his region appeared to be going well.

This wasn't happening by chance. Like any good chief, Philip was very aware that he had to keep a firm eye on what was happening in the world outside the "villages" in his region. He knew that if the change program was to work, he had to quickly demonstrate benefits to customers and business improvements to his bosses.

Working closely with a small group of change enthusiasts from both East and West, and with people in headquarters, Philip had started the process of designing the new product range. Given that he was from "the East," he had made special efforts with the "West" to ensure that his people there felt the benefits of being part of this group and supported in their roles. For Ian, a country director from West Africa, this was already a big improvement on the old arrangements:

> I felt enormous relief actually . . . in various ways. Although it is far removed from the days of steam liner and the telegraph, those country director jobs are quite isolating. Having more communication and more support available I think was a genuine benefit.

Those in small operations had been afraid of being swallowed up by a big, new region where they would simply disappear off the radar. To counter this, Philip made sure these countries had his attention, as Binte from Senegal describes,

> It was natural to have that kind of fear, especially if your country is small. Philip understood and, funnily enough, it turned out to be the opposite.

So, yes, there was progress. But, we had evidence that despite our efforts so far, this was not yet a team. People were still not spontaneously linking, pooling resources, or creating solutions to common problems. There was something more required if we were to achieve a deeper level of buy-in and create a level of regional teamwork that could drive the organization forward and be sustained over time.

A couple of days before the Addis Ababa meeting, riots were reported following the disputed Ethiopian election result, with the arrest of thousands of students, teachers, and opposition political leaders. Despite uncertainty about whether the meeting could go ahead, and the continuing advice to check the British Foreign and Commonwealth Office website, all seemed well at the moment we boarded the plane.

We arrived in a grand marble palace of a hotel set far back from the street. The thin air of high-altitude Addis Ababa meant that climbing stairs left you embarrassingly out of breath. A day trip out to the Blue Nile Gorge gave us a glimpse of the rural Ethiopian Highlands. Our expectations were turned upside down when we saw field after pretty field of harvested grain neatly stacked and ready to be brought to market. In contrast, Addis was more difficult on the eye: donkey carts on the streets, exhausted women carrying small bundles of sticks for firewood having walked many kilometers simply to earn a few coins. From a distance, we saw armed troops racing to break up a riot, abandoned buses, and uniformed pupils locked out of a school. Like Douala, it struck us once again that this was the business environment in which these teams in the organization were doing their work day after day, week after week.

Somehow, the trip out made what we had to do inside the conference room seem a little easier and underlined the real worth of the work we were doing to build the strength of this group. While Ben and I were at the Blue Nile Gorge, Philip spent the day rushing from one premeeting to another. Since Douala, Philip had created the Regional Steering Group—a small group of senior managers taken from within the Regional Leadership Team—whose role was to oversee progress on the merger and change program and to give advice to Philip on the way forward. We had agreed to have a premeeting with Philip and this group as part of the preparation for the workshop.

When we caught up with Philip for a few minutes before sitting down with the Steering Group, he seemed quite wound up and distracted. He was dissatisfied because in spite of the progress made in terms of business results, the group of 30 still did not feel to him like a real team. For the last 12 months, we had been dragging and pushing them: Now we needed them to unleash their energy, realizing the benefits of working together.

Given this ambition, the Steering Group meeting did not get off to the most promising start. One member began an animated argument with Philip saying, "It's all about trust. That is part of your role Philip not to frighten people about possible job losses. You can feel their resistance building." Nevertheless, Philip was uncompromising about sticking to corporate targets for impacting more customers and becoming more cost effective. To his by now sullen and switched off colleague, Philip reemphasized the fact that the targets were given and the team needed to work together to make choices about how to deliver them.

Ben and I pressed on to brief Steering Group members to stay out of adversarial squabbles in the 3-day meeting with the group of 30 and instead we asked them to build on the special role they had started to play as coaches in Douala: being alert to any defensive behavior, listening, questioning, and summarizing to bring real issues to the surface. We expected from what had just happened that some would find this difficult.

What I did not realize until later was that, in the run up to the meeting, Philip had been reflecting hard on his role and impact on the group. During this time, he had a significant insight—"One head does not contain all the wisdom"—that meant he wanted to make a shift in his leadership style. He no longer needed to push the regional agenda so hard as he could now channel regional funds to where they would have the most impact. His finance director had prepared a single page financial spreadsheet (jokingly called "the thing of beauty") for each of the 11 countries, and which when added up, gave the total budget for the region for the next 5 years. Instead of holding this close and trying to push and command the change, Philip had decided to open the books and offer it to everyone, then to coach (instead of "tell") his people on how to use this information to move the business forward. This shift in Philip's approach made a huge difference to what followed.

As the group of 30 assembled the following morning, they seemed ready to get down to business and by lunchtime were quite upbeat, but the afternoon proved more difficult as participants challenged one another to get creative about how to achieve tough new targets for raising new income and reducing costs. Philip and his immediate staff instead of pushing people became a "coaching resource" called on to clarify "the thing of beauty." Effective though this was, by mid-afternoon, energy levels were dropping as people were getting worried about whether they could reach the targets and unsure about whether they had the capacity to deliver the new products.

By this time, we didn't think that the group would be capable of producing much from the day, but the closing plenary at the end of the afternoon surpassed our expectations. Feedback from the team showed that not only had the "thing of beauty" been understood but it was also accepted and liked! While the afternoon had been difficult, the penny had finally dropped that the region had only a finite amount of income available at this point. Most now understood that they needed to organize their resources in a much "smarter" way and in collective agreement in order to deliver the required result. They had made a big step toward taking shared accountability for action and results. One of the country directors summarized the change of heart that the team had experienced:

> We've realized this afternoon that we are all in the same boat!

It was a magical moment, as if the group's identity suddenly changed before our very eyes: They were no longer the territorial hippos we had become used to!

In spite of some unanswered questions, this was a major result, both in terms of a strategic agreement to budgeting but also in terms of team personality and strength. That evening the Regional Steering Group worked very effectively in reviewing the day and taking decisions on certain outstanding questions, which were announced the following morning. Philip was disappointed that the wider plenary of 30 had been unable to take these decisions, but he acknowledged that he had been unrealistic and with the Steering Group providing a bridge between him and the group of 30, everyone seemed finally to be getting into their stride.

The following day, we gathered round and began by reviewing progress toward regional working and we received an interesting comment from the group:

> This should have been done at the beginning of a meeting because each time there is a little bit of progress to celebrate and we all need to recognize the special contributions that some people are making to this.

At first, hearing a criticism of the program, my reflex was to be defensive and justify the sequence of the workshop but hearing the "we" in the statement and the desire for recognition of a shared venture from the group was very encouraging and reinforced our sense of an emerging team mentality.

For the next 2 days, we continued to work on developing the regional products interspersed with some physical "social mapping" activities designed to provoke people in the group of 30 into forging links with colleagues in other countries.

During a break, one of the African senior managers reflected back to us that part of the group enjoy sitting down discussing while another part "enjoyed being out of their seats, moving, being expressive." As facilitators, we had catered for these preferences with a good mix of activity and talking in the program. Looking back, however, we noticed that the older, more set-in-their-ways country directors were comfortable expressing themselves in the rough-and-tumble of strategic roundtable discussions but awkward in activity that was at all expressive or playful. They wanted to get on with the "real work" of discussion while others were freed up by breaking out into different modes of interaction.

The inability to shift styles seemed not only to betray a lack of understanding of their "real work" as a leadership team, but also to arise from an entrenched hierarchy. Back at home we imagined the old-fashioned country director "telling" but terribly nicely, filling the air with clever speech, while unwittingly or presumptively stopping a colleague from speaking their mind, yet achieving this pleasantly enough to hold an "inclusive" illusion in place.

When toward the end of the meeting, Wambui, a senior manager from East Africa, took Philip aside and said,

> It's good that the African senior managers are here but you do realize that many of us still don't feel able to fully participate in this meeting and this needs to be addressed if this team is really to work.

This seemed to make inescapable the contrast between the easy rhetoric about "being inclusive" and a not-to-be-referred-to "hierarchy of contribution": If you were a woman, African, or lower in grade, you generally spoke less. As feedback, it felt painfully true, and there was a realization that in spite of all our efforts as facilitators some issues were still not on the table.

Nevertheless, the meeting ended on a high. Instead of a typical close for the workshop—pulling together a joint action plan—we decided to ask pairs from each country to share "a single action they had passion to implement" on their return. As we went round the room, the energy seemed to build from one person to the next like a series of firecrack-ers. People were bursting to speak and confidently declaring quite radical things they intended to go back and do. One director declared, "It is time to clear the decks and get started on the new agenda." Another committed to complete a difficult reorganization before the next meeting. Philip had prepared closing words but put them aside. He was delighted and did not want to add anything. It was as if the whole group was smiling.

People gathered around Ben and me at the end expressing their appreciation for a great meeting and conveying their recognition that something special had happened over the last 3 days. They were now part of something exciting and new—a leadership team—and this was some-thing that they could draw strength from when they went back into their country operations with difficult actions to take.

By the end of the Addis meeting, the team had decided to operate as a region, balance the books, and support one another, while holding coun-tries accountable for their performance. This was undeniable progress. Mark, the skeptical new arrival at Addis, had revised his opinion:

> The advent of the concept of a region suddenly made a huge amount of sense in terms of economies of scale, cooperating in a kind of multilateral sense rather than working country by coun-try where our programs were very small. Previously, there was no coherence to any of it. It didn't add up to a story.

Yahya from Ghana, who had painstakingly explained to us the impor-tance of pecking order and strong hierarchical leadership in Africa, had now experienced the benefits of working as a team:

> You have to create an environment where you have people expressing an idea, moving away from the position of thinking "I don't want to do anything wrong" to being creative and utilizing the resources that we have. You need a leader who gives you the political support to push an idea through, for setting targets and sticking to them. There is an old saying that "One tree does not make a forest." The leader has to be quite good at carrying everybody along.

The facilitator–leader collaboration between Philip and me had taken a big step forward during the Addis meeting. We were finding how to work more effectively together. Afterward I asked him about this and he replied,

> As a leader who is willing to take risks, I tend to see an opportunity or a space and then push fast toward it, but the people I need with me will often close up or block. What the facilitator does then is to embrace the others who are switching off wherever they are and as the facilitator inquires, they soften and the space opens up differently so that you as the leader are not on your own anymore. They are there with you.

I have noticed that ideas come up fast for Philip, he races toward them and sometimes he leaves others behind. While he is operating like this, they cannot step up but in Addis the shift he made, stepping back and listening more meant that people became more engaged, as if responding to his trust in them.

Nevertheless, in spite of the breakthroughs we had made, the comment from Wambui about senior management participation still hung ominously in the air. Yes, we could make a strong argument that we had become more inclusive but was it good enough? What made it more worrying for me was a sense I got of a refusal to speak about how the targets and decisions agreed at our meeting would actually be communicated and implemented back in countries.

Ben and I went home uplifted by the energy in the closing session and pleased at the progress we had made but I was troubled by the fact that one year after our first meeting in Nairobi there were still "elephants in the room." I wondered if I had been too caught up in the mechanics of facilitating. Did I need to spend more time speaking with individuals to find out the stories and struggles they had been unable to express in public? Yes, the sun had come out after the Douala rain but somehow I still felt that if I looked over my shoulder, storm clouds were hanging worryingly on the horizon.

How Do You Approach This Phase?

We needed to bring people together after the disturbing effect of Douala. Linking back to the fable, Philip, like the young chief, was realizing that he needed to take a different path. He knew that he wanted to galvanize the group so that they could achieve "real teamwork" and make a difference. He realized that continuing to push and provoke was not going to deliver this but it was unclear to him at first exactly what sort of shift he needed to make.

Moving On

Having said goodbye to the past, how do you align your team toward a common goal for the future? Janice Prochaska (Prochaska et al., 2001) describes a five-stage approach—*pre-contemplation, contemplation, preparation, action, and maintenance*—to align attitudes and behavior in individuals.

Initially, a leader like Philip is "ready to get on with it" (in action), bringing a change to someone who "has not thought about it yet" (in pre-contemplation), and the yawn they receive is not the reaction they hoped for. The temptation is to get angry, frustrated, and push harder for the breakthrough. This is where the leader has to fight their instincts. Instead of pushing, the leader needs to set aside time for the team to work on weighing the options and making their own mind up.

The next job of the leader is to explore realistically with the team both or many sides of a question and work through their defensive reflexes (freeze, fight, flight) that stop them addressing the question. This is called contemplation and here the leader can push, both challenging and sup-porting the person's exploration and they can expect strong emotional reactions, as at times a person may feel unloved, rejected, angry, hurt, threatened, and vulnerable. The leader should not be disappointed if, at this stage, the person fails to behave rationally or proactively. This is normal! Each person is torn apart by opposing instincts: to pull away suspiciously in fear or to advance trustfully or excitedly and embrace the new.

In many mergers, the discomfort of contemplation is prolonged until the moment when a new layer of jobs is announced. When a person recognizes the "choice point" (e.g., choosing whether to apply, whether to accept a job offered, whether to take a package or a new direction), they move from being "lost" to "found," and their new identity emerges, bringing joy, relief, and a new sense of excitement. By the end of contemplation, the penny has dropped and a person is ready to move into making plans for what's next (preparation).

Preparing for Action

Having been through the pre-contemplation and contemplation phases of Prochaska's model in Nairobi and Douala, most participants arrived in Addis with the penny having dropped, recognizing that the merger had happened and that regionalization was under way. In Addis, they entered the third Prochaska phase, preparation, in which a person intending to make change grapples with the practicalities of that change. They can feel deterred if they experience the resistance of others but on the other hand, if sure of themselves and well supported, they can also be strong role models for others by showing they are on board and buy in to the change.

Creating a New Sense of Identity

Work by a Chilean biologist neuroscientist, and philosopher, Francisco Varela, helps us to recognize the significance of the moment when a leadership team says: "We are all in the same boat." To use the term coined by Varela (Maturana and Varela, 1988), this is a moment *autopoiesis* that signals the emerging of the team's new emerging identity. Every living system maintains a boundary, even though all its components are in continual flux. Varela says this is how a living cell "bootstraps itself out of a soup of chemistry and physics" (quoted in Goleman, 2003, p 306). The whole organism that emerges cannot be explained by the individual elements. What he describes applies this to all levels of life from a single cell to the immune system, the mind, and even to whole communities.

Giving Birth to the New We

In a healthy organization, people feel a sense of significance and belonging: Each department or team is simultaneously *well differentiated*—they know who they are—and well integrated—they are well linked with teams upon whom they depend (Oshry, 1996). A merger or change program disrupts this.

Philip had experienced many times before the feeling of a real team around him but had been frustrated that it hadn't happened sooner in this case. Tony, who has facilitated mergers of teams in many other situations (including hotels, hospitals, pharmaceuticals, finance, and telecoms), knew how to form a team from a collection of individuals, but had also been surprised about how long it had taken to occur in this merger. Neither had taken sufficiently into account the challenges of distance, culture, and the additional problems associated with the constant turnover of staff in the group.

Both of us had noticed that there are special moments—in fact the true moment of a merger—when a team's new identity emerges like a protective bubble around a group of people.

There are three important things that the leader can do to propel these aligning moments:

- *Share* the key information ("the thing of beauty").
- *Challenge* the team to face the threat. When the problem starts to weigh heavily enough on a group of people, they eventually unite around it, provided they feel the trust of the leader in them, as this expands their confidence.
- *Support* each person in the team to feel significant, competent, and trusted (Schutz, 1994), including giving objective feedback on results and encouraging each person to build on these. When a person feels positive about who they are being (their personal "identity" in a group), this spills out positively in their behavior toward others, making everyone in a group more confident and flexible.

If the leader encourages each person to make lateral connections with each colleague, and in this to discover how they can help each other in addressing the threat, then this multiplies the speed at which each person's frustration and fear transforms into courage and a sense of excitement.

Releasing Passion

Larry Hirschhorn, a leading exponent of psychodynamic consulting, describes how the defensive patterns of an organization arise through extreme anxiety or insufficient leadership. He works shows how the kind

of passion expressed in the final Addis session is a way of unleashing positive energy and getting the organization back on track (Hirschhorn, 1999).

An organization answers the "What are we here for?" question with
a "primary task." For Toyota it might be "to make and sell cars," but for
Philip's organization it was "cultural relations." Any challenge to the way
the primary task is delivered brings certain risks to staff—to their comfort,
physical and psychological health, safety, relationships, prosperity, and survival. The leader's job is to contain and spread this risk through clarity,
certainty, rules, and structure, so that staff can step up to responsibility and
achieve a deep sense of engagement and fulfillment. If the risk is not properly contained, staff become overwhelmed with anxiety, which they seek
to contain through "social defenses" (e.g., time wasting, talking about easy
topics instead of the real work, inflexibility, inefficient work processes).

When the primary task of an organization changes from say, being an air-
line to a train operator or from being a donor to an enterprise organization,
the risks entailed in changing provoke massive anxieties and social defenses.
Hirschhorn points out that when people find passion in the new primary
task, this gives a limitless source of energy, removing anxiety, unraveling
social defenses, and providing a great capacity to endure difficulty.

What Are the Signs of Progress in This Phase?

1. When individuals are seriously preparing for change, grappling with
   the practicalities of "How?" rather than contemplating whether or
   not to go forward. When individuals are showing signs of commitment and the effect is spreading (Prochaska).
2. When the group is uniting against a common enemy or challenge
   (in this case "working on the regional budget") and starting to experience the strength and identity of the group (Varela).
3. When individuals and small groups find an action they are passionate to implement on behalf of the organization (Hirschhorn).

What Are the Tools You Can Use?

In this third phase, the three tools that follow give the leader ways to
engage others in addressing these key questions: What information do we

need to share? How will we take decisions and create accountability? How do we connect up across the team?

No 1: "The Thing of Beauty"

The people who need to contribute to a team result need to know both the overall team result that they are seeking to deliver and the contribution others expect from them. Initially, the shared task of the leadership community is something the leader knows a great deal about and may be somewhat burdened by. Their challenge is to find a way to express the shared task concisely in facts and detail and show individual members of the leadership community what they must contribute to produce the needed overall result.

In Addis, Philip and his finance director crafted a single sheet of paper that contained all the necessary information. This "thing of beauty" was used by subgroups to challenge and support each individual, thus to clarify how to make their contribution.

This clear, factual base to discussions made possible the change of heart in which members of the group of 30 discovered that they were "all in the same boat," interdependent and reliant on one another. Shortly afterward, this led to autopoiesis and the sense of being one team.

No 2: The Steering Group

The people who take decisions need to be well connected with those who have the key information as input into those decisions. After Douala, there was a yawning chasm between Philip and the group of 30. Philip expected the group of 30 to take decisions but they were showing no signs of being willing to do so.

As an interim measure, we engaged five members of the group of 30 (a mix of East and West, old and new) as a sounding board for Philip in setting the agenda and judging how hard to push on any particular point. Before the start of the Addis meeting and at the end of each day, the Steering Group met with Philip and the facilitators. This provided an opportunity to review progress and set priorities. At times, the Steering Group were able to take decisions and report back the following day, thus spreading the leadership of the region beyond Philip into a slightly larger group as a step toward wider ownership by the group of 30.

No 3: Social Mapping and Swarms

Each person in a new team or network is a source of information for the others, yet it takes time and encouragement for connections to form. After Douala, we noticed that the connections we expected between the 30 leaders had not yet materialized.

We asked them to count the number of meetings (face to face, telephone, or email) they had held with colleagues in the group of 30 over the last 6 months. Then, they wrote the three figures on the flipchart and we could all see how many emails had been sent and how few phone calls they had made. The powerful conclusion was "We must pick the phone up and call each other more." We then asked each person to draw their social map, first as an inner circle containing the three people of the 30 with whom they communicated most.

All members of the group went to stand in an open space with three long pieces of string and handed the other ends to the three people in their inner circle. This showed us which individuals and which countries were the hubs through whom most communication went, and who was poorly connected on the periphery of the region. After this, we reflected on how many links are possible in a network of 30 (And we calculated that the answer is 435!). The power of the network is realized when all those links are made. This showed people the potential of the team and how, by making more connections, everyone would benefit.

Finally, we enacted a moving simulation of a swarm (as in a flock of birds or shoal of fish) to represent a network of colleagues operating under two different conditions, the first supportive and the second hostile. Each person was to choose two others without letting them know. Under the first condition, they were to continue moving silently to maintain equidistance from their two people with a powerful, flowing motion and smiles on their faces. Under the second condition, they were to choose two more people and to label one the bomb and the other the shield. They were to continue moving silently to keep themselves safe, with the shield always protecting them from the bomb. This time the movement was fast and jerky, more exciting that the first condition but also more chaotic and stressful. We reflected on the trustful style of relationships they needed to generate, in order for the team to be both enjoyable and highly productive.

What Is the Evidence of Completing This Phase?

- The leader feels relief and progress.
- The leadership community is united in a new identity, bonded, engaged, and confident: "We know what we need to do."
- The leadership community is ready to move the change out and down across their teams, and feedback is reaching them from all parts of the surrounding organization.

The key aspects of Phase 3 are summarized in Figure 5.1.

Tips

- Take a few minutes to recognize what has been achieved. Acknowledge the progress you are making, but don't get seduced by the magic of the breakthrough moments. Also remember the challenges ahead. What has not been resolved by the leap forward? What do you need to focus on next?
- Have some customer success stories up your sleeve to share with your team, to underline what really matters in your business—the customer. It helps the team focus on the outside world not just the anxieties of their internal change world.
- Share some failures too. It makes the successes seem more credible and your team will appreciate the honesty.

Phase 3. Leadership Community Falls Apart... Then Steps Up

Action: The community falls apart then regroups as a team

Tools
• Thing of Beauty
• Steering Group
• Social Mapping and Swarms

Sign of progress?
• Individuals are grappling with the practicalities of how to change
• Members are uniting and enjoying the strength of the group
• Individuals find an action they are passionate to implement

The challenge
For Leader: *How do I transfer ownership?*

For Community: *How can I engage myself and influence what is happening?*

Focus questions
What do I know?
What do you know?
How do we take decisions and create accountability?

Evidence of completion?
Leadership Community are bonded, engaged and confident. *"We know what we need to do"*.

Leader feels relief and progress.

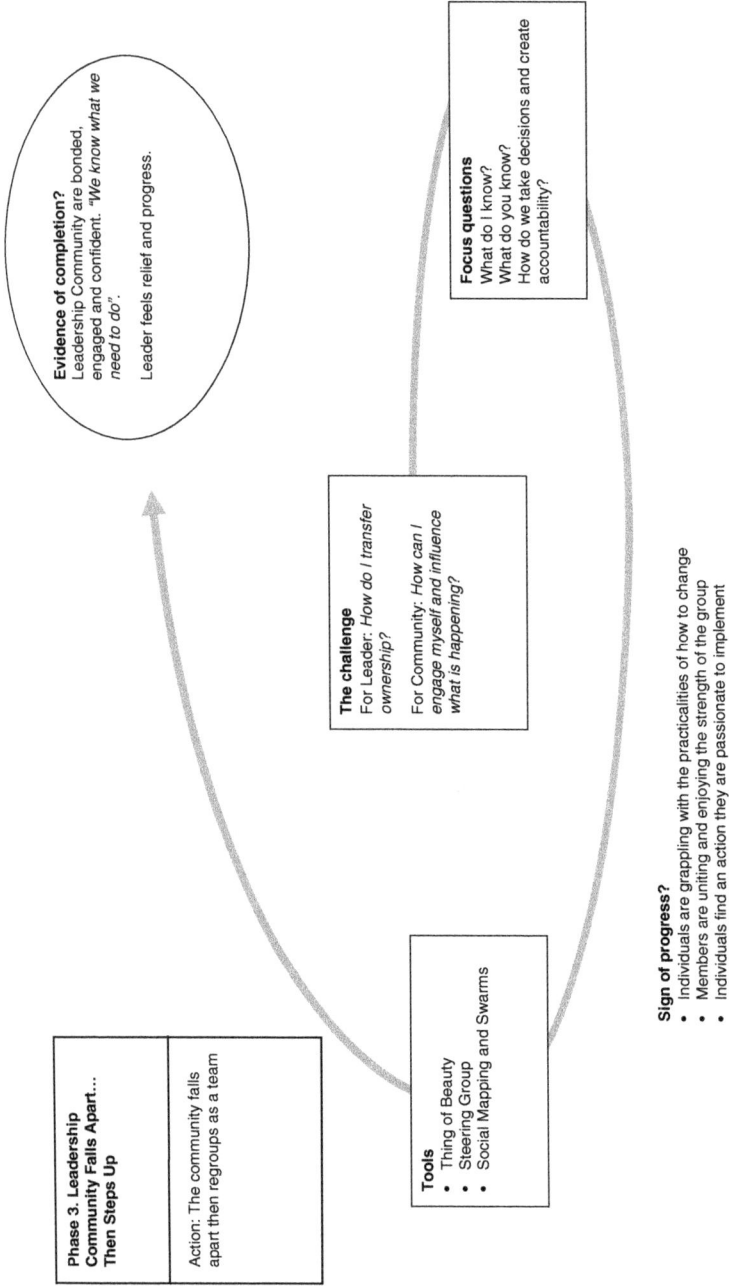

Figure 5.1 Phase 3 summary

CHAPTER 6

Fourth Phase: People in the Wider Organization Pull Back Then Embrace the New Reality

The Fable (*continued*)

What the chiefs least expected when they returned to their villages was to suffer the young chief's problem. Their people had lost confidence in them and rejected the call to change, saying, "You have betrayed us and we no longer trust you."

Word had reached the young chief and from afar he stepped in. He asked each village to send a representative to a special meeting where the chiefs would listen to the concerns of their people.

The people's representatives returned from this meeting saying, "We have voiced our fears . . . but the danger is real and it is not the fault of our leaders. They do not have all the answers and we must play our part in tackling this together."

With renewed faith the people were ready to plant the new seeds and fight back as one.

The Challenge

Suddenly it's as though the floodgates have opened. The leadership team buys into the change and is enthusiastic to take it back to each of its members' teams. To their disappointment, their teams reject that call. The leaders' new enthusiasm leaves them cold, feeling betrayed and angry. How do we restore their confidence?

Philip: Our Story

Since we had left Addis Ababa, Wambui's reflection on the way the leadership group was interacting was nagging away in my mind. It wouldn't go away. At the start of the merger, I had set out with the lofty intention of removing hierarchy and releasing the energy, commitment, and capacity of the team of 500. Ensuring that the entire group understood and contributed to the future shape of the organization was something I passionately believed in before taking over in East and West Africa. But thus far, I had only done this with smaller teams. I wasn't clear or confident how this would come about in so large a team spread across 4,000 miles and 11 countries. Nevertheless, I felt it was essential if we were to create a sustainable improvement in business performance.

For the previous 12 months, I had focused on engaging the leadership team—getting them to understand the need for change and trying to work through our different responses to the challenges in front of us. Tony and Ben had helped me make a breakthrough in reaching that group of 30 and there was a growing feeling of joint purpose and team identity. After Addis, there was a real sense of elation in reaching a peak that we had been striving for. Now, I had this very real doubt about the strength of our achievement. Yes, my immediate leadership team were moving forward but was it far enough? And what about my wider team of 500? Where were they?

In travelling around the region, I wasn't convinced that we were communicating effectively on the change. Yes, in some countries you could see leaders were actively communicating with staff. For Otim this was a new responsibility:

> I had to do a presentation to all staff. There were some anxieties that jobs may be cut. We needed to reassure people and explain that it's good for us to work in a new way. Obviously some were skeptical and there wasn't 100 percent buy-in at the beginning. It took time to sit down with people and explain to them what it meant.

In some countries, effective communication was producing real improvements in delivery but often I could feel a resistance in staff or even a simple lack of knowledge on why the organization was changing and what we were trying to achieve.

When I arrived in one country, staff used my visit to start a "work-to-rule" because of a dispute with management. Before I flew in, I had been forewarned by one of my close colleagues in Nairobi that this was likely to happen, but worryingly, the country director was taken by surprise. On the way to the office from the airport, the country director was urgently ringing people to find out exactly what kind of action was being taken. When we got to the building all was quiet but staffs were wearing black and red armbands as symbols of protest. It was a desperate effort to draw attention to their concerns and to the fact that they felt their voice was simply not being heard. As I came down the stairs, I met a delegation sent to talk to me. It was intimidating and I felt slightly cross at being cornered in this way, but to defuse the situation, I suggested to the group that we convene an all-staff meeting in an hour.

At the meeting, I simply sat and listened. I was clear that I was not promising to solve their issues at this point but I was willing to hear their concerns. As I visited the other offices in the operation, I repeated the same offer. Staff seemed glad of the opportunity for discussion and it succeeded in reopening the potential for dialogue between management and staff. There was clearly a huge amount of hurt and misunderstanding on both sides.

While this is an extreme example, it was symptomatic of communication problems I had noticed across the region, but overall, my leadership team didn't agree. Then came a deafening wake-up call! In the annual staff survey carried out by MORI, the scores showing levels of confidence in our leadership have fallen significantly. It's a big disappointment but it confirms what I feared. Yes, the leadership team is on board, but so far, we or they have failed to reach the wider staff back in countries. The worst result in the region is from our largest business—Nigeria—with 40 percent of the region's staff.

The truth is that in our heart of hearts, we have all known this issue was present but so far had left it in the background. Now, we had a great opportunity to get our team to look—as a group—at the issue of wider engagement. I could use our next leadership team meeting to raise some challenging questions: How do we engage the 500? How effectively do managers and staff relate to each other? What is it that blocks communication, creativity, and innovation? What is it that leaves people stuck in a cycle of low performance, productivity, and dependency?

We had to get the problems—whatever they were—out on the table in order to spur the team into a new way of working. Yes, we could carry on as we were. It was certainly better than where we had started 12 months before, but it was still far away from our vision of a high-performance team. Alternatively, we now had the chance to press ahead through some very choppy waters toward another step change in performance. We chose to push on.

Working with Tony and my head of human resources, we mobilized the 11 African members of the leadership team each to interview five staff from a cross section of levels and departments in their own country to find out what makes them feel confident in their leaders and what gets in the way. We also asked the 11 country directors to interview three people asking the same question, and the head of human resources to interview a handful of staff across the region. Through this approach, we reached 98 of the 500 staff—almost 20 percent of employees.

But what on earth would come up from this research and how would we be able to deal with it? Was this going to be our Pandora's box? The issues were deeply sensitive: Not only were we talking about relationships between country directors and their teams, but also issues between UK-appointed and African staff. We knew as a British organization working in Africa, we had the legacy of the United Kingdom's colonial past to negotiate. The biggest cop-out would have been to avoid the sensitive issues but confronting them meant entering a minefield where we needed to be "inclusive" and hyperaware of the pitfalls that arise from engaging in difficult conversations across cultures, about race, and between groups and individuals in different positions of power. We mustn't fall into the trap of generalizing or stereotyping. It would have been much easier to avoid all this, leaving in place the barriers to performance. While carefully designing our approach to the coming meeting, we consulted closely with our organization's Equal Opportunities and Diversity Unit based in the United Kingdom.

The meeting was due to take place in Lagos, a chaotic megalopolis of around eight million people in Nigeria. It's a place of high energy, of charged emotions, where people speak their mind, tempers flare quickly and just as quickly quieten down again. It was the perfect metaphor for the days ahead.

Although we were staying in an international hotel, major rebuilding works were going on next door to our meeting room and our conversations took place against the noisy backdrop of drilling. Twice, water pipes burst in the ceiling overhead filling an empty champagne bucket put there for the purpose and breaking the tension by causing welcome laughter among the group.

So how did we choose to address Wambui's question on senior management participation in the meeting? Tony and I took the controversial decision of splitting the group for a day—country directors in one room, other senior managers in the other. It was a risk. Would it reinforce the divisions that were already there? How would this be interpreted by the two groups? Would it alienate country directors?

We felt that it was a risk worth taking. Wambui's feedback had hit home—hard. We wanted to get staff voices into the room without distortion and without being suppressed by the more experienced and influential country director group. We had to build the capacity of the less senior members of staff if they were to have genuine influence on the meeting. If they didn't have that influence, we would simply not be able to move to a new level of performance as a team.

With the African senior manager group, we spent a day looking at the research. What did it tell us? They took turns to share their findings from each country with their colleagues, and as people listened to each other, the experience was empowering. As Binte from Senegal said,

> I kept asking myself 'here am I standing in front of colleagues and they see me as someone they can seek guidance from.' It helped build my capacity.

How could this group best present the messages back to the country directors? The group had not only found many common issues but also the courage and determination to present their findings clearly and in a balanced way. They were not naïve: While knowing this was a unique opportunity to expose the real issues, they risked an adverse reaction and needed to plan carefully what to say. All played a part.

Meanwhile country directors worked on the issues blocking our ability to deliver the change program. When we came back together, the country directors surprised the African senior managers by presenting an imaginative and playful analysis of the challenges we were facing in our capacity to deliver. They made a clear commitment to communicate the vision, clarify expectations, bring resources, create openness, and empower staff. They underlined that failure to do this would ultimately mean closure, while on the other hand, success would enable everyone to deliver relevant programs and interesting jobs. So far, so good.

Then it was the turn of the African senior manager group to provide feedback. The session that followed was uncomfortable. You could hear a pin drop. For the first time, the whole group (including country directors) was really listening well. The feedback was direct, personal, and emotionally charged. It started positively. The African senior managers' first point was that they valued the vision, the sense of direction, and the willingness to work as a team to address the points they were about to raise. Then Foluke from Cameroon stood up to communicate staff concerns. This was her first leadership team meeting and, initially shy, she soon found her voice in giving feedback to the leadership team on issues that were personal and highly contentious:

> You seem indifferent, aloof. You don't say hello. You don't reply to emails. In short, it feels like you lack respect for us.
>
> You are secretive, you fail to consult, and present decisions badly. In short, we feel taken for granted.
>
> You overload the capable staff and condone poor performance.
>
> We need to modernize the management–staff relationship from one that feels like master–servant to one of two-way, mutual accountability, with feedback in both directions.
>
> On pay and conditions we need rigor, transparency, and staff involvement.

Foluke's clear delivery of these points contributed to the deeper shift in the leaders' attitudes and behavior that was to follow.

Next the country directors were asked to respond. Quite a number were simply stunned. There was silence suggesting very mixed emotions. For the African senior managers, there was a sense of exhilaration as some deeply felt concerns were finally being expressed. They had finally won the attention of the country directors and their voice was fully present in the room.

Instead of provoking a bun fight, we decided to pair up each country director with the senior African manager colleague from their own country to review the findings and identify and explore in greater depth exactly which aspects applied to them. We could see that some pairs were getting straight down to this while others were having difficulties. One country director simply avoided sitting with his colleague! Another bursting with anger said that this approach had been "wrong" and "too negative": "I felt doors slamming in my face." Blinded by a red mist, he failed to notice that he was talking all about himself while his country colleague, an African senior manager, was ignored as he sat patiently beside him waiting for the storm to pass.

After the allotted time, the country directors asked to be given the chance to respond as a group.

There was a hush in the room. One country director simply thanked the country-appointed staff for what they had said, acknowledged the importance of the issues, and asked for time to consider his response. Others were uncomfortable with the emotional nature of the discussion and tried to depersonalize and rationalize what they were hearing. Anthony, for example, stood up and said,

I can see what you're saying. Actually, there is a taxonomy of behaviors here and I think I can see a new model of leadership that we can draw up.

Francis, on the other hand, was angry and not liking what he was hearing. He started to question the process:

Hang on—where did you get this information from? Why is it confidential? I'm not sure any of it's true anyway and I think presenting it anonymously in this way is simply unfair to us.

Although the country directors had asked for the floor, finding themselves under the spotlight in this way was a lot to cope with. The conversation lurched unpredictably between hurt feelings and clumsy attempts to recover.

A long, meandering but moving discussion followed with the African members of the team telling stories from their research about the impact of leader behavior, highlighting cultural differences, for example, in the way people say "Hello." People were bursting to speak but the individual contributions didn't connect with each other, as though each person was on their own with their emotions, venting and thrashing around. The conversation became frustrating to listen to and it looked as if Tony was finding it tiring to facilitate. On the positive side, people were no longer finding clever ways to reject the findings, but were now struggling as if to digest some exotic, unknown food. While in each case the speaker was earnest, they were not yet a team taking responsibility. An hour passed and the conversation still had life but it was not clear where it was going.

The most heartfelt issue was the paralyzing effect of decisions and conversations avoided, particularly those that relate to staff who were not performing. But above all, what worried me as the conversation went on was that a chasm seemed to be opening in the room leaving the African members of the team as victims of a bad former colonial power. Then Yahya from West Africa proposed a practical action that began to heal the rift:

> If a director phoned a few people up to speak to them personally they would be so delighted, so confident and he could have so many supporters!

Mark, a country director from East Africa, seized the moment and built a bridge with his honest disclosure:

> I know how bad some of you feel, because I've also felt badly treated by the organization at various points over the years.

This surprising contribution drew the group together again in common cause. As the afternoon came to a close, things still felt inconclusive and "up in the air," and in the goldfish bowl atmosphere of the meeting, I found myself exasperated. I felt that we were still avoiding some of the issues. Ben was exploding with impatience, wanting to blow up the entire group, and this was when we nicknamed him "Mr. Dynamite"! Tony, who had been holding the space as facilitator for the entire afternoon, was exhausted, but seemed to accept the need for people to vent and explore before taking responsibility. Despite the frustrations, he was confident all was OK, but he was wrung out and seemed barely able to continue speaking! With strong emotions still swirling around, everyone needed time to reflect—often in private and not just overnight but in the days and weeks ahead.

The next day we asked each country director to work with their senior manager in country "pairs," thinking through plans for how they should respond to the feedback in their country operations and how they would communicate the discussion with their teams. We also completed a quite different topic on prioritizing our key stakeholders, which served to switch everyone's attention back out of introspection into the external delivery challenges we faced.

In a coffee break, Tony and I were relieved to see new and spontaneous mixing among the group with different clusters forming instead of the usual obvious cliques. Tony told me that conversations seemed more open, and he noticed that it was easier to draw ripples of laughter from the group. Personal chats with a few people had taught him more about previously unmentioned challenges faced by staff, including the difficulty of speaking about their personal performance, the isolation of the country director role. He reported one African senior manager had received death threats while introducing a new company purchasing system! We were bringing skeletons out of the cupboard, and there was no going back. We could expect the word about this meeting to spread fast to all staff and success now depended on the leaders showing they had listened and changed their behavior.

In spite of the difficulty of the conversations, this meeting was a critical step in getting all senior managers to a common understanding of the issues and barriers to engaging *all* staff in the change process. As Otim, an African senior manager, said:

> This open and frank discussion led to change in the way people behaved and the assumptions they made, which I thought was extremely positive. It opened the way for us to work together, irrespective of who you are, and it created a fundamental and positive impact for the region.

During the course of the meeting Ian, one of the country directors, had picked up some strong and affecting stories:

> It revealed an awful lot actually about some things that needed to be uncovered: directors who went into their office and never said "Hello"

to people; some people feeling that they had to kind of psyche themselves up for 15 minutes in their car before getting out of it and going into work. So there were some really quite deep issues of morale and feeling among some staff that through a brave move Philip unearthed and those issues could then be talked about and dealt with.

In my closing remarks at Lagos, I took the opportunity to thank Ian, who was due to move back to the United Kingdom, for his significant contribution to the region's work over the past 18 months. Ian's support in the early part of the merger had been vital, both for his practical work in reducing the product range and for his personal support helping to enroll West African and smaller countries into the new enlarged region. Spontaneously and with real affection, the others in the leadership team responded to my few words with a standing ovation, leaving Ian shuffling from foot to foot in embarrassment.

This poignant moment marked the end of an era in this team's life. We had just made a difficult crossing and having got safely to the other side, now we had to say goodbye to someone who had helped get us there. Everyone had appreciated Ian's hard work and he had the respect of the entire team. It made me reflect on the key qualities I valued in Ian and other colleagues in positions of authority over the years. It seemed to boil down to this: integrity, commitment, and service to the group rather than the self. All of these had come to inform my sense of what a leader could and should do.

Looking back, the meeting had exposed senior managers, both country directors and their African colleagues, to staff opinion. This helped UK colleagues to better understand the cultural context to the feedback and to start thinking through how they could work together to engage staff. The process also empowered the African managers and encouraged them to take joint responsibility for responding to staff views. This was a major step in getting our teams to work together to address deeply felt and long-standing barriers to change. Yahya used a word picture to describe how important this meeting had been for keeping all members of the leadership team together:

When the river is travelling downstream you have to be careful to ensure that the front water does not separate from the back water.

When this starts to happen, before long the stream dries up. It's as simple as that. So you make sure you carry everyone, all members of the teams, along together.

Otim describes how this meeting finally brought African senior managers on a par with their UK counterparts, creating new opportunities for them to lead change in the region:

> Previously, it wasn't recognized for us to sit on senior management teams and things like that. But now we do have, as we speak, a number of senior management posts that have been created across the region and staff who can contribute at that level actually filling those posts. That was something very positive that came out of that meeting. We recognized what we can do together as a region that can create impact and also we learned that we've got talent in the region. It doesn't matter if you're African staff or UK appointed, we can contribute equally together and create impact. We removed some real and serious divides between African and UK-appointed staff.

Word spread quickly among staff about the conversations that had taken place at our meeting and the commitments to change from management. This was the opening of a door. You do not change 70 years of working practice overnight, but Lagos was a symbolic ending of an old way of relating. It gave me, as the leader, a platform on which to hold others accountable to a new way of working and through some simple behavioral changes on the part of the leadership team, confidence in our leadership increased significantly. In the global staff survey undertaken by MORI the following year, our results were not only the best in our organization but also matched figures of top 10 performing companies, both private and public sector, in the United Kingdom. This included extremely high positive ratings for statements such as the following:

- I have confidence in the management team running my country.
- Staffs are consulted. Change is well managed. I am informed.

- I am aware of improvements arising from the last survey.
- I understand the contribution I am expected to make.
- Training and development is helping me to develop skills I need in my job.

Although we had taken a risk with our approach to this meeting, it had paid off, finally delivering a fundamental shift in the way we worked together as a team.

How Do You Approach This Phase?

The story of this stage in the change process is particularly challenging. As in the fable, the chiefs had gone back home and been rejected by their people who felt betrayed. Observing this had happened, Philip wondered how he could form a "distance repair" without disabling the chiefs and making things worse between them and their people. How do you successfully bring difficult and emotionally charged issues to the attention of senior managers? And, even more tricky, how do you get them to engage positively with these issues when they potentially challenge their sense of humanity and integrity in dealing with others?

The Power of Stories

We wanted researchers to gather stories and to use these to unearth the issues that needed to be addressed. While working at the World Bank, Stephen Denning tells how through trial and error, he discovered and developed storytelling in order to galvanize the organization's knowledge management activities (Denning, 2004). Denning educated himself in how others, from Aristotle onward, have used storytelling. He was particularly interested in discovering the narrative power of a traditional story and its limitations in the context of an organization. Some stories are boring, some need to be open to provoke people to think, some need to be upbeat and positive to motivate, while others are powerful because they are unashamedly negative and illuminate a problem that needs addressing. Inspired by Denning, we designed the research to collect both positive and negative stories.

Reconciliation of Interests

Nevertheless, we were concerned that as people received negative stories during the workshop they might start to feel sorry for themselves—feeling unloved when they receive criticism or incompetent or badly looked after by their organization—and that they might collapse again into victim mode. Alternatively, they might swing into over compassion for staff and fail in their duty to the organization. We needed a way to call people to their responsibility as leaders, recognizing their accountability both to the organization and to their individual members of staff. Charles Handy, one of the leading thinkers and writers on organizations, defines leadership as "combining the interests of individuals with the collective interests of the larger community to which they belong" (Handy, 2008). The effective leader needs to reconcile those interests if the organization is to succeed. Understanding those interests and achieving this balance, is a central leadership dilemma and one that leaders need to resolve in each decision they take. We shared Charles Handy's definition as we introduced the workshop and carried it as a reference point as we facilitated the discussion, constantly asking ourselves, Are both sides of the leadership dilemma being expressed in the room right now and how are they coming together?

Having Difficult Conversations

We anticipated that after the stories had been presented, and the country pairs had worked together on the feedback, there would be a need for a large group conversation in which the whole plenary made sense of the sometimes difficult topics being raised and the larger process of change they found themselves in. But what sort of conversation did we need to have and how should we facilitate this?

David Bohm, a leading quantum physicist, later in his life devoted himself to the practice of "dialogue." He distinguished "dialogue" from simple "discussion," which he likened to a ping-pong match in which we hit a ball back and forth between us, normally with a purpose to win and only occasionally accepting part of another person's point of view (Bohm, 1990). The purpose of dialogue is to come together as colleagues, going beyond one person's understanding, suspending assumptions, embracing contradictions and confusion, and achieving a common meaning. The focus is bringing to the surface and altering the tacit infrastructure of thought.

Bill Isaacs and Peter Senge working at Massachusetts Institute of Technology (MIT) have built on Bohm's work to turn dialogue into a practical method. They find that such conversations go through various crises, or "hot moments," where extreme views provoke distress in others (Isaacs, 1999). Provided people pay attention without falling victim to their strong inner reactions, they are able to reach a deep "crisis of collective pain" in which thinking takes on a different, slower pace, with a deeper sense of connection. Out of this connection, new solutions emerge and become possible. Central to the success of dialogue is what Isaacs describes as "the container," which means creating a setting that is sufficiently safe and clear so that it is possible for participants to discuss a topic that is dangerous. Tony and Ben's role in providing this container was critical. As Ian, one of the country directors, emphasizes,

> In terms of getting commitment from people and bringing them together, Tony and Ben's facilitation was useful in that process. It would've been more difficult for Philip to do it by himself or for us to do it, so it was critical to have external facilitation.

Deeds Speak Volumes

When the whole group dialogue in Lagos had reached its natural conclusion, we asked country pairs to identify behaviors and actions they needed to take on their return to their workplaces. Most people were tired. Some were quite disorientated and concerned about the quality of the action plans they were preparing. We asked ourselves what we should be looking for from our leadership team. John Kotter says,

> Deeds speak volumes. When you say one thing and do another, cynical feelings can grow exponentially . . . The guiding team says we too are being asked to change and, like you we won't get it right immediately, we need your help and support . . . people love honesty, it makes them feel safer (Kotter and Cohen, 2002).

This is what we needed from our team—simple and highly visible behavioral changes coming out of the meeting that would signal with bright lights, bells, and whistles blowing that something positive has happened and a shift has occurred.

What Are the Signs of Progress in This Phase?

1. When staff members bring both positive stories (demonstrating confidence and support for their leaders) and negative stories (indicating a lack of fear and a desire to create conditions for success) to their leaders (Denning).
2. When all in the leadership community understand the organization's purpose and how they can contribute to and benefit from success (Handy).
3. When the difficult interpersonal issues are out on the table and the different experiences and expectations of individual members are heard, and in doing so, the group strive collectively to overcome the issues raised (Isaacs and Senge).
4. When the leadership community commit to simple actions and behaviors that will build confidence and respect in the workplace (Kotter).

What Are the Tools You Can Use?

In this fourth phase, the three tools that follow give the leader ways of engaging others in addressing these key questions: What do you want from me? What do I want from you? To be more specific, What leader behavior helps or hinders staff confidence? What issues do leaders need their colleagues to hear? What simple improvement actions and behaviors will leaders commit to?

No 1: The Staff Research

Following the staff survey, we needed to find a means for staff to raise their real concerns and to have these addressed by their leaders. However, staff felt insecure and concerned that they might pay a heavy price for speaking out. We designed research that protected confidentiality and encouraged honesty.

Each member of the leadership team interviewed between three and five members of staff in their country. We provided questions and a format for the interviews covering the following:

1. Examples of behavior that give you confidence in the leader
2. Examples of behavior that take away confidence from the leader
3. What good things your leaders are doing already
4. What you would like your leaders to do more of or less of
5. How could you step up yourself as a leader to provide a more positive environment for others?

After the staff research, we brought together the African senior managers for a full day to analyze common themes, find their voice, and prepare to present the findings back to country directors.

No 2: Rackets

We might promise we'll go to the gym to keep fit, but we stay late at the office to finish our emails instead. We know we should go to bed early but we lay reading social media messages on our phones even though we know that is going to keep us awake. Often, as human beings, we promise ourselves and others that we will do the right thing but something stops us. We call what kicks in and stops us from doing the thing we are committed to do, a *racket*. This is because, just like the mafia, we get a "pay off" for stopping something happening. Our seemingly irrational behavior benefits us in some way or is more convenient. The cost for letting ourselves or our colleagues down may not be obvious or we may simply choose to look the other way.

The more aware we make ourselves of our rackets, the less chance we have to get caught in them. That is why we invite leaders to reflect on these four questions and to explore their answers with a colleague:

1. What is one commitment I am not achieving despite effort?
2. What am I doing instead?

3. What do I gain from this avoidance?
4. What are the costs of this avoidance?

No 3: The Stories—Talking in the Round

The staff research and feedback left the country directors feeling criticized and they wanted the "right to reply." So, we arranged 11 chairs in a circle and the rest of the group sat round the edge. The country directors were invited to hold a conversation among themselves in the presence of the wider leadership team. After initial comments from each country director this became a very open dialogue involving the whole group of 30. One person spoke at a time while 29 people listened intently, both to the words and to their deeper inner reactions. The facilitator's role was simply to receive contributions from individuals, giving them time to say what was important, until after about 2 hours the dialogue naturally came to a close. This provided the opportunity for people to get things off their chests, to explain past misunderstandings, some of them culturally based (e.g., "You might think when a Nigerian says 'Hello' a second time he is simple—this is not the case . . ."). The session rebuilt the relationship between country directors and their African senior managers, and later sent ripples out to the wider staff. Afterward, the team conversations were more two way, more "in the same boat as fellow human beings" with less hierarchy or formality.

No 4: The Action Plans

Following talking in the round, we thought it important for each country to commit to an action plan that would both communicate the research findings to local staff and put in place the necessary corrective actions. Country pairs were to spend the final hour completing an action plan with a named person responsible and date beside each of the following:

1. Circulate research findings to all staff
2. A personal response thanking each interviewee
3. A "stepping forward" meeting of the country management team
4. An all staff meeting reporting back from Lagos

5. A feedback meeting for each leader with their direct reports
6. A change committee in each office
7. A regional vision workshop, including progress to date and gaps to close

What Is the Evidence of Completing This Phase?

- Staff have spoken out on issues that concern them and the leadership community have actively listened.
- Leaders have got over the feeling of "You don't love us anymore; we're angry with you" and come to a point where they recognize "We need you if as an organization, we're going to survive."
- The leadership community has identified how their own behavior is an obstacle to staff engagement.
- Staff recognizes that they and the leadership are "in the same boat." They have moved from mistrust to a recognition that "You are in a difficult position too."
- Leaders and staff commit to specific positive behaviors that they are prepared to sustain, for example, saying "Hello," knowing people's names, explaining decisions, and raising issues constructively.

The key aspects of Phase 4 are summarized in Figure 6.1.

Tips

- Give people time to digest. Make sure your influencers in the group know what is coming. Make sure managers have room to respond. Facilitators need to manage this carefully. There is a serious risk that the bad news from staff turns off your senior managers. They become defensive or try and avoid the issues.
- Find the heartfelt actions—giving emphasis to simplicity and commitment.
- Seek advice from those in your organization with responsibility for equal opportunities and diversity. Dealing with management–staff issues is a sensitive area.

Phase 4. People in the Wider Organisation Pull Back... Then Embrace the New Reality

The Leadership Community become the initiators and struggle to engage their people

Tools
- Staff Research
- Rackets
- Stories-Talking in the Round
- Action Plans

The challenge
For Leader: *How do we engage the wider team?*

For Community: *Now I'm enthusiastic why is my team not?*

Evidence of completion?
Staff speak up on issues that concern them

Leadership Community actively listen and respond positively

All recognise that they are "in the same boat"

Focus questions
What do you want from me?
What do I want from you?

Sign of progress?
- Staff members share with their leaders both positive and negative stories
- All leaders understand the purpose, how they can contribute and benefit
- Difficult interpersonal issues are on the table.
- Leaders commit to simple actions and behaviours to build confidence and respect in the workplace

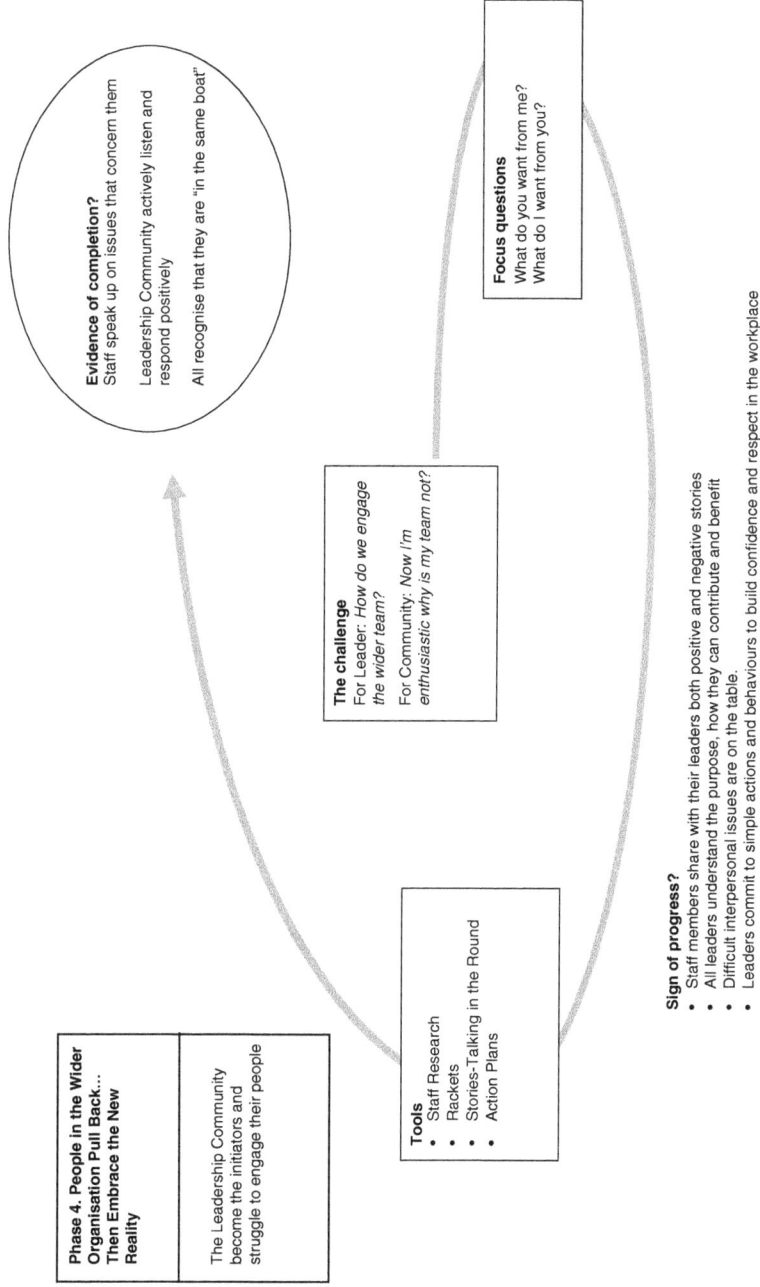

Figure 6.1 Phase 4 summary

CHAPTER 7

Fifth Phase: Identity Shifts and the Rubber Hits the Road!

The Fable (*continued*)

As they started to work together—chiefs and villagers, East and West—a remarkable thing happened. The villagers looked at their reflection in the lake and the chiefs were no longer thick-skinned like hippos. They were no longer divided between East and West and the people were no longer blind. They had been magically transformed.

What had they become? Not slow elephants nor tall giraffes nor crafty hyenas, but animals that were faster and more cooperative. The chiefs said, "We have become like gazelles," and the people happily responded, "Yes we are lean, adaptable, and ready to run energetically together to find the best pastures."

Since that day there has been a new confidence, with women and smaller tribes also contributing their voices alongside others. The people suffer less as they face up to reality, create solutions together, and are leaders influencing each other. The young chief is no longer needed and has moved on to be a chief in another land.

This story of hippos, lions, and gazelles is now told to all the young gazelle children and acted out in their games. Before adulthood, each child learns how to turn themselves into a lion and how to deal with any territorial hippos they might meet, just in case.

The Challenge

There is a new sense of excitement, possibility, and achievement. We're being recognized for our success in introducing change. With people on board we now have an opportunity to raise the bar and tackle some long-standing and ultimately life-threatening issues. How can we engage the whole team and realize their full potential in addressing these issues?

Philip: Our Story

Things are really starting to move! During the last 6 months, the wider team of 500 has really come together and there is a noticeable sense of team identity built on the successful delivery of a range of ambitious new products that are recognized as having potential in the wider world beyond our region. The staff survey figures have vindicated the risks we took in Lagos and have boosted the confidence of the leadership group.

Just before our last team meeting in Lagos, I received a request in feedback from staff to write a regular monthly email updating them on progress we are making across the region and how we are tackling the challenges facing us. I had resisted doing this before, feeling that somehow I would be adopting a leadership pose and *voice* that wasn't my own. But since the feedback was honestly and bravely given, I felt I should respond. So, for the last 6 months, I've been writing a short monthly message to all staff and it surprises me how positive the response is. I ask people to get in touch if they want to comment on issues or ask questions, and amazingly, some do. It seems to reduce the distance between us, bringing the East and West Africa team together within its new identity. It reflects me finding a stronger voice as a leader.

We also introduced a recognition scheme across the region. Every 3 months, we give cash prizes to members of the team who have helped us to deliver on our change plans. The scheme was set up so that over the year, we can expect 25 percent of staff to receive bonuses and recognition for their contribution to our work. Every 3 months, an email goes out to all staff announcing the winners and describing how they helped us to deliver change. There is huge enthusiasm from staff for this initiative and I get lots of emails from winners saying how excited they are at being named and how it is inspiring them to do more.

All this told me we were in a strong position. We are delivering a new level of performance and impact, as Otim, one of the African senior managers, describes.

One customer said to me the other day, "I've known your organization for many years from the tiniest little thing to this huge thing." That was his comment but we've never changed numbers: We've always been less than 25 people in the office . . . but his perception of our organization is that we have become this big thing, doing a lot more!

There is a sense of unity and purpose across the business and I'm starting to think we have momentum in all parts of the organization and I'm no longer having to push. For the first time, I feel that the leadership team of 30 is really confident and secure in its role. As Akello says,

> Myself I feel like I'm more empowered to do things because I now have that challenge of saying "I must prove to myself that I'm able to do this" and I'm always looking for the best result I can produce.

The leaders are trusted to act by their teams and by me as regional director. This in turn gives them a strong license to operate. I could easily just let this carry on under its own steam. What exactly is there for us to do now?

It's going through my mind that time is running out for me as a leader of this group. I probably had 18 months left in the job and I'm wondering, "Am I satisfied with where we've got to? Have I really achieved what we needed to?" I'm also asking, "What on earth should I do after that 18 months? What is the next challenge for me?" With these questions in mind, I ask Tony for some leadership coaching to help me clarify next steps.

Shortly, after one of these coaching sessions, I'm sitting in a taxi on the way to work. It suddenly comes to me as a flash of inspiration. I'm struck by the fact that while we've made some very significant changes, particularly in developing a strong product range and engaging the team across the region, we haven't yet taken the opportunity to address some of the deeper, underlying issues that hold us back as an organization.

I know the team is much more receptive to new ideas and ready to engage with them. Why not use the new found energy, confidence, and commitment of this group as an opportunity to radically redraw the boundaries of our organization? This is a chance not just for a series of incremental shifts but for a big leap forward.

That morning, I work with some of my colleagues to come up with some new default positions for the organization—a set of 10 givens— simple descriptions of how we will operate going forward. The idea is that with these we will draw a line in the sand, delineating the shift between the old and the new worlds of our organization. We then have a brainstorming session on what we think are the few significant areas of challenge for us as an organization. We end up with six including the reviewing of our business model, expanding our customer base, demonstrating the impact of our work, and improving our levels of customer service. There is a wonderful sense of energy in the room, and amazingly, this is the work of just a few hours.

Some days later, I ring Tony and tell him that this is what I want us to focus on in the next leadership meeting—harnessing the newfound belief and enthusiasm of the East and West Africa team to understand and respond to these six big challenges facing the organization. The leadership team will redefine the way the East and West Africa business operates and delivers. It is a chance for them to really lead the change. If we pull it off, we will finally be delivering leadership across and down through the team. Weeks before the meeting, we ask the leadership team to organize themselves into one of the six challenge areas that appeals to their interest and strengths.

When we get to the meeting in Dar es Salaam, Tanzania, we find that we are staying in an incredibly beautiful hotel overlooking the harbor. We have a meeting room with natural light. There is a great bar on the eighth floor. People are in an excellent mood and there is a real sense of pleasure at being back together again. This is evident in the first session where we review our journey as a team over the last 2 years. Emotions emerge, of pride and surprise, at how far we've come as a group, and so does a stronger sense of identity. This is most palpable for the new members arriving in the team.

We have planned to ask each of the six challenge groups to find their passion for tackling their challenge area, to work out what the most difficult issue and core dilemma is, to describe the step change that we want to achieve, and then to agree on two actions that they will take responsibility for delivering over the next 6 months, making themselves accountable to the leadership community.

On the first day, Tony and Ben keep reminding us of the need for equal voice and they seem to have stepped up a gear with dynamic plenaries that draw more and more energy from the group. It feels like a convection current of positive power that is building up within the team. As the day comes to a close, we are upbeat. Then, unexpectedly, while a few of us are reviewing the day, a strange argument breaks out between two country directors, Chris from Sierra Leone and Gail from Ethiopia. Chris expresses concern:

> Let's be honest. What we're doing here is a sham! After this meeting, the African senior managers all go back into a hierarchy. We are pretending we are empowering them but not really. What are we empowering them with?

Gail, who had previously confided her frustrations with the rough and tumble of our earlier meetings ("Although I was allowed to speak, I was not really listened to"), bursts out in frustration:

> It is patronizing and untrue to say we are not working as equals. Just look at the reality of those African senior managers who are taking on team leader roles on behalf of the group. What do they say? Just look and listen to the evidence. Our people out there are seeing and feeling the difference on the ground!

The exchange touched a nerve and took us briefly back to the issues of Lagos. At first I felt a bit anxious about the strength of these emotions but as the discussion continued, it became clear that actually Gail and Chris were in violent agreement.

Chris's concern was based on a fear that what he was seeing grow in this meeting—passion, commitment, confidence across the team—would simply evaporate once we returned to our offices. Although he sounded skeptical, it was as though he was checking in with others on their levels of commitment. Gail, who was finding the meeting liberating for her and her senior manager, fervently wanted to hold on to something that was clearly working for her. In speaking up with such enthusiasm, Gail was able to reassure Chris that the commitments we had made in Lagos were shared, deeply held, and sincere. Thankfully, the following day, progress continued and Gail told Tony how far the team had come since she joined in Addis:

> At first I felt there was no space for me in a leadership team dominated by men, but now this feeling is totally gone.

As the team continued to look at the core dilemmas confronting the organization, we were brought face to face with the uncomfortable truth of having no easy options. Tony and Ben were really pushing the group not to gloss over the issues but to take time to understand them deeply and to make sure that the whole leadership team understood the problem well enough to be receptive to any solutions they came up with later. For some, this was too slow and they wanted to move on because they felt the issues were obvious. But getting people to connect profoundly to the problems is an essential part of focusing their energy to solving them.

Just when things seem to be going very well, Tony and Ben hit us with an uncomfortable question: "What makes a person most influential in this team?" They ask us to stand in order of how much influence each of us feels we have on this group. We shuffle around a bit and settle in a semicircle with me (as regional director) feeling rather on my own at the high-influence end. What followed was interesting. First, we talked a bit about why people were standing where they were standing. I learned that many felt just as uncomfortable as me having this hierarchy of influence exposed so starkly. Then, shockingly, in spite of all our progress since Lagos, someone noticed how uneven the circle was. And, yes, when you looked it was true: Those near to me were more likely to be from the East, male, white, UK appointed . . . and the proportions shifted as you went round.

Suddenly and worryingly, we were returning to Chris's concerns of the night before. Then, as we began to explore this circle of influence with the group, Otim from Kenya and Sanyu from Tanzania, two African senior managers, who had been in the middle of the circle, spontaneously walked to join me at the high-influence end. Otim declared to everyone:

> Sanyu and I just talked and said, "we know what we need to do and we are not going to wait for others." We have decided to put

all of our energy behind the work that we are doing in this work-shop and we recognize that we have a real opportunity to influence the big decisions the region is taking. It is up to us to take that chance. That is why we are moving.

Immediately standing next to these two colleagues I felt much less lonely. Again the expectation and sense of hierarchy was challenged from within the group. Taking the cue from Sanyu and Otim, Tony concluded the session by asking each of us to figure out how we can both influence others more and allow ourselves to be influenced by others. We discuss this in groups for 5 minutes before continuing with our task.

While this had not been comfortable, the exercise had exposed a number of powerful points. First, it reminded us of the risk of complacency creeping into a team when you think you have tackled some difficult tasks. For us, this was particularly true around issues of equality of voice. There was always the risk that inequality drifts back into our way of working through laziness or lack of attention. Second, Otim and Sanyu had shown us how individuals need to take their chance to create influence. Once again, team members had shown courage and woken the rest of us up to our responsibility.

For the rest of the afternoon, we keep going back into plenary in order to get whole group buy-in to the different directions we might take. Each challenge group then has to trust the other challenge groups to do work on their behalf. This last part is a particular challenge. Too often in the past, senior managers were blocking actions across the region because they felt they had not been closely involved in the decision-making process. Given the size of the region and the challenges we faced, the team needed to accept that it was impossible for all of us to be involved in decisions in all areas. Colleagues would need to work on issues on the organization's behalf. If they were to be effective and empowered in doing this, all of us (including me as regional director) needed to give up some of our authority and let them get on with the work. This is why we spent so much time on the sign-off process for proposals made by the challenge groups throughout the meeting.

The tone of the meeting continued to be challenging but positive. Then, suddenly we hit another snag. One subgroup, overconfident from the positive reception to some of their earlier ideas, misjudged the mood of the team and suggested a "big bang" approach to staff change that left the meeting angry. Their ideas were rejected as "arrogant" and "bullshit." Three amazing things happen. First, the subgroup gets this feedback very directly from the wider team. Second, they show incredible strength in taking that feedback constructively. They go back, rethink, and re-present their ideas taking into account the views of the leadership team. Third, the leadership team as a whole shows emotional maturity and a collective sense of responsibility by consciously making sure that the subgroup are drawn back into the leadership team as a whole and don't feel left behind. There is an added sense of solidarity as a result and watching this take place, I almost want to jump up and down. I feel so proud to head up this organization!

As the days go by, the sense of momentum is growing. It's like we've moved into fifth gear after having been stuck in second for a long while. There is joint action, responsibility, and purpose in the room. Everyone seems to be engaged, sleeves rolled up, addressing the challenges and their new tasks.

As the Dar meeting draws to a close, instead of being tired people seem inspired, more confident than ever that they can rise to the challenge. This represents a shift in the identity of the group of 30 as they recognize themselves contributing in new, more significant ways and with a renewed sense of purpose. It's as though we all grow a bit taller, because we're proud of what we are achieving.

Tony and Ben ask the group of 30 to describe who they have been this week. Almost for the first time, the group recognizes their power and responsibility as they say,

> We have been leaders not managers because we have been decision makers, focused, critical and challenging, inclusive, taking responsibility, listening, evaluating, empowered, and setting policy.

By the end of the meeting, the burden is shifting from me as leader to the leadership community as a whole. When I convene the Steering Group for a postmeeting review I am bowled over by their enthusiasm. Mark says, we "got to clarity." Thomas says, "We are suddenly in the business of being a region." Gail says, "For the first time I feel we're going home with the tools we need to work with." And it was Chris, who 3 days earlier had said this was "a sham," whose attitude was transformed:

I have seen genuine empowerment and while I am still skeptical—
that is my nature—I feel what you could almost call enthusiasm;
I almost want to burst out in delight . . . !

Chris paused midsentence to recover, and then we moved on to agree
on the message and next steps we would take away.

Many of us attending the meeting are leaving on the same plane out
of Dar es Salaam and the mood is buoyant. Mark, enjoying his newfound
clarity, is reflecting on how this new sense of alignment has been created:

We don't have a grand strategy that will fix everything. Instead of
setting out to answer a very big question with a very big answer
that doesn't really work, we start out with that very big question
but then you start producing a whole series of incremental answers that move you forward, keeping you flexible as you go. That
is the right way to develop an organization.

We take off over the Indian Ocean and head north to Nairobi passing
over the snow-covered Mount Kilimanjaro. I later see this scene played
out on a video that had been made of our meeting. It looks great! It's
certainly never been easier to write my monthly all-staff email reporting
on what we have achieved. I sign it off:

I was inspired by the willingness and ability of the leadership team
to take responsibility for leading us forward in meeting the challenges we face and to do so quickly and decisively.

Following this meeting, I hear more positive reports. For example,
Otim reflected his excitement at the role he was now playing, having
decided to put all his energy into being a positive influencer:

Now, just picture this scenario: I am a locally appointed member
of staff and I'm meeting country directors who are senior to me,
and this team of country directors and regional people who are
way above me, but I am leading them and getting them to do
work to address income levels in the region!

Akello, who in Nairobi had been worried about how the region would contribute to her local office, had taken a much bigger view of things having taken on a regional coordinator role:

> The merger has brought me new areas of responsibility. For example, I manage a particular program with managers from 15 other countries to do with trust building between communities. For me, getting people to accept me doing that and having a growing sense of confidence made me feel very happy that the change program had actually happened.

After the Dar meeting Gabriel, a country director from West Africa, found the courage to address long-standing issues of poor performance, giving staff the choice to apply for positions in the new organization or to move on.

> Some of these issues were about people being set in their ways. A lot of people knew they needed to be resolved. Now we've dealt with it and you're kind of free from that baggage. The most overwhelming thing has been the energy and attitude from the new team, although they did lack experience, the attitude has been a complete 180 degree turn. The atmosphere is different. It's like a different organization.

One of the country directors had suggested before the meeting that we make a video of the discussions as a way of communicating with the whole of the East and West Africa team. This inspired move captures the energy and positive mood of the leadership team for all to see.

Watching the Dar video and noticing what was unleashed there, I'm enormously satisfied because I know we have delivered what the rest of the team of 500 require of their leadership: courage, decisiveness, and integrity, and that there is clarity, confidence, and commitment across the organization to what we can achieve.

How Do You Approach This Phase?

In the early phases of the merger, we constantly felt as though we were dragging the group and they were slow to find their own energy. Now, finally, the group seemed not only aligned with one another but also in a trusted position with their people back in country; in other words, ready to lead. We needed them to bring their passion to the life-threatening challenges and find solutions that would move us forward and in doing so, the group needed to become the gazelles of the fable—lean, adaptable, and ready to run energetically together to find the best pastures.

Self-Organizing to Motivate People

Harrison Owen, a management guru who has organized conferences all over the world from small West African villages to global corporations, has developed a method for larger groups to self-organize in a highly energetic and productive meeting around any issue of shared concern (Owen, 1997). This method called *open space technology* includes one law, the so-called *law of two feet,* which says, "If any person finds him or herself in a situation where they are neither learning nor contributing, they must use their two feet and go to some more productive place." This reminded us to give people choice about which topic they work with and the opportunity to express to others their passion for their chosen topic. Once people had chosen to work on a particular topic and given the choice to switch groups, their levels of commitment and motivation increased.

What's the Real Dilemma?

When confronted with a challenge, it is often easy for a group to gloss over the difficulty of the choices that they face. On the face of it, what is the dilemma in customer service? Do we provide lousy service that generates angry, upset customers or do we provide excellent service that leaves customers surprised and delighted? The answer seems obvious but offers no real sense of why this group had previously been unable to deliver.

Each life-threatening issue was difficult to address because it contained buried and paralyzing dilemmas, that is, choices where both options seemed bad or both options good. For example, to close a service outlet is bad because it denies access to customers but to leave it open is also bad because it consumes budget. Charles Hampden-Turner looked at the problem of reconciling dilemmas and showed that when people work with a dilemma a third option typically emerges that combines and transcends the other two (Hampden-Turner, 1990). Of the many ways he describes to approach this—including mapping, contextualizing, sequencing, combining —we chose simply to ask participants to present the dilemma as two, mutually exclusive and difficult, options A and B. When the large plenary group gave their feedback on the options, this proved extremely useful in opening up a new way forward for the group as a whole.

To help the team find their position in relation to the dilemmas confronting them, we drew from a family therapy approach called *constellations*. This method developed by Bert Hellinger is also powerful in organizations (Hellinger and Ten Heovel, 1999). It involves people being physically assigned to stand in a position in the room. The position they stand in represents through distance and direction their relation to other parts of the larger system and from this position they report how they feel and why. This physical method inspired us to understand people's views on the dilemmas and for everyone to literally vote with their feet on the direction we might take. It also sparked various activities we used to make the workshop highly dynamic and energetic, including the influence circle, lineups in relation to the dilemmas, and a "walking in the dark" exercise to sensitize the group to issues of letting go and trusting others to work on their behalf.

Who Are We Now?

Richard Pascale, a business school professor, has researched the subject of corporate transformation, studying companies that have succeeded in fundamentally shifting their ways of operating, including British Airways, Honda, and Ciba (Pascale et al., 1993). He realized that fundamental transformation is not achieved simply through doing. What people do at work arises from an operating paradigm or a set of assumptions tied in to their identity. A shift in the identity of the company or "who they are being" is needed before a new operating paradigm can be made to stick. When we asked the group of 30, "Who are you being right now in this workshop, and who are you going to be when you get back to the workplace?" they answered, "We are the decision makers." Asking this question seemed to capture and internalize the positive and energetic spirit of the workshop. It provoked what Francisco Varela called *autopoiesis* or emergent identity (Maturana and Varela, 1988).

Remembering the lack of action after the Nairobi workshop 2 years earlier, we were very concerned to create conditions for participants to be really mobilized and to be doing things differently after they had finished the Dar es Salaam meeting. Gerry Johnson is a professor of strategy who has studied strategy workshops, comparing them to rituals found in other walks of life (Bourque and Johnson, 2008). He says rituals—including primitive rites of passage, marriages, and funerals—involve a separation from everyday life and a kind of performance, bringing symbolic communication, strong emotions, and the ability to cause transformations. There are three stages: *separation* from old identity, an in-between *liminal* period in which there are images of death and rebirth, and then finally, a *reintegration* into society in a new status.

Johnson's research highlights the success of strategy consultants in the first two phases but also shows that consultants are less successful in managing reintegration. A simple action plan does not have sufficient symbolic power. He suggests a series of workshops may be needed and better preparations for the emotional not just the cognitive challenges when participants face the dilemmas of applying the strategy back in the workplace.

As a result, we spent more time tapping into passion as a sustaining energy, surfacing the real dilemmas within the workshop, building trust and consensus in the leadership team, clarifying and signing off actions, rehearsing a single communication message to take back, and making explicit the groups' shift in identity. The video was an incredibly powerful tool not just in communicating back to the team of 500 but also as an aide-mémoire for the leadership group, reconfirming who they had become through the story played out on film.

Two Doable Actions

Harold Sirkin and colleagues at Boston Consulting Group (Sirkin et al., 2005) studied change programs taking place in 225 companies and discovered a consistent correlation between success or failure around four key factors—*duration, integrity/capability of the team, commitment, and effort*—making the acronym DICE. Put simply, short duration projects run by capable teams backed by commitment of leaders and staff and requiring little additional effort by staff to implement, these types of projects succeed. Each factor can be simply quantified and an unsurprising but often overlooked key to project success is to arrange things so that staff need to put in no more than 10 percent extra effort above their day job.

Typically, in the closing stages of a workshop under considerable pressure to commit, people make long lists of actions. A key to our success in Dar and beyond was to ask each group for only two concrete, doable actions that they were confident they could deliver on before the next workshop in 5 to 6 months.

What Are the Signs of Progress?

1. When individuals recognize that if they are neither learning nor contributing, it is their responsibility—not that of the leader—to find a place where they can be productive (Owen).
2. When the group face up to the really difficult dilemmas and are able to transcend those difficulties to find a way forward (Hampden-Turner)
3. When individuals in the group recognize how they achieve influence within that group and beyond (Hellinger).
4. When the group is able to recognize a shift in their identity—who they are being—by putting it into words (Pascale).
5. When the group is able to commit to actions, openly owning responsibility for delivering on those, and able to describe how that will happen in a realistic way on returning to their workplace (Johnson).

What Are the Tools You Can Use?

In this final phase, the five tools that follow give the leader ways to engage others in addressing these key questions: "What is the reality of the big challenges we face? How do we build momentum and confidence in the team?"

No 1: Finding Your Place in the Story

One of the new members of our leadership team told us that arriving in the group was like coming into a cinema when the film was halfway through. If they were going to make sense of what was going on next, they needed to understand what had happened in the bit they had missed.

Each time we brought the group of 30 together, there were some new faces appearing and some familiar faces missing. To get us moving quickly and purposefully in the meeting, we discovered that to spend 60 to 90 minutes bringing everyone up to speed with the story to date was very valuable. We introduced the new people, asked them to pair up with existing members and to catch up with the story by reflecting on the experiences and lessons gained in the earlier phases of the story. Insights were posted on wallcharts and played back to the group.

At the end of this, each person knew the others in the group. They had caught up with the plot, and the achievements of the whole group had been remembered and celebrated.

This honors a principle called *self-reference* (Wheatley, 1994) whereby a system is strengthened and freed up to change by keeping a memory of its evolutionary path, out of its past history into its present identity, as a reference point for change. This has proved an enormously powerful tool in building a new team identity.

No 2: The Givens, Survival Challenges, and Groups

Philip as leader worked with his immediate colleagues to identify the givens: these were a set of clear guiding principles that as leader he needed to make plain. For example, as a matter of policy, library space will close. These principles helped the entire team to understand the shift and reposition themselves—not simply to rearrange deck chairs on the ship but to construct a completely new ship, going on a very different journey. With the givens stated, it was possible to articulate a small number of life-threatening problems that team members needed to address. We identified six survival challenges: income, impact, structure, customer excellence, outreach, and brand. Team members were invited to self-organize into six equal-sized groups choosing a challenge to which they were motivated to contribute.

No 3. Dynamic Plenaries

The Dar meeting alternated between small group work and plenaries in order to gain whole group input and sign-off for the small group work on the survival challenges. This alternation could have become boring had we not challenged each small group to be highly engaging and creative in maintaining the energy of the meeting. Quickly they learned that debate in plenary is draining, so a practice evolved where after their presentation, a small group would invite questions, but instead of batting back answers they would simply note the questions and take them away as feedback. Other devices included "Everyone stand up until you support the direction proposed then sit down"; "skits" on customer service; "a marketplace" for selling solutions; "gallery walks" to share information; "speed dating" to make deals with colleagues; and 2-minute "elevator pitches" for a punchy persuasive sell.

No 4. What Is Our Identity? Who Are We Now?

We realized that at Dar the group had been working together in a very different way as leaders of the region. This shift was evident to us but we were not sure if it was evident to everyone in the team or whether it would be easy to sustain when they got back home. We asked the group to answer a couple of questions: Who are we being here in Dar? Who will you be when you get back to your countries? Their answers served to confirm to all that they had taken on a new identity here. They had become leaders taking decisions on behalf of the region and they wanted to continue holding on to this identity on their return to their country operations.

No 5. Bringing It Back Home—The Video

Back in their countries, people would be waiting for the leaders stepping off the plane to find out what had been decided: Do I still have a job? What is going to happen now? What did you talk about? But it would be difficult for anyone to convey all the insights, messages, decisions, and above all, the spirit of the meeting. That is why at the Dar meeting, one of the country directors decided to make a video, catching key parts of the discussion, interviewing participants, and showing the range of issues discussed. At the end of this, he produced a 10-minute video including reports from all six challenge groups. A copy was provided to each country.

What Is the Evidence of Completing This Phase?

- The group stops prevaricating and dancing around and finally grips the issues in their entirety.

- The group is able to organize themselves into work teams and to make and take forward decisions on behalf of and accountable to the leadership community, deciding on new ways of working appropriate to the new situation.
- There is a shared sense of momentum, confidence, and inspiration—a pride in who the group are and what they are achieving.
- The group is able to define its identity as a leadership team and to communicate that to the wider team for which it is responsible.
- The burden of decision making shifts from the leader to the leadership community as a whole.

The key aspects of Phase 5 are summarized in Figure 7.1.

Tips

- A short video is a fantastic communication tool particularly in conveying the personality of a meeting but make sure you have a storyboard before you start filming. If not, you are going to have hours and hours of editing ahead of you.
- Congratulations! You've built a strong sense of team but make sure new members joining your group are not overwhelmed by the robust identity of your group. Pay attention to how new team members are integrated and welcomed if they are going to get up to speed quickly and feel included.
- Support and mentor the work groups once they are back in the workplace. Stay in touch. Encourage them to keep in touch with each other. Recognize what they are doing and help those who encounter obstacles to overcome them.
- However much progress you make, the job is never completely done. Realistically there is always the risk that issues and habits you have tackled creep back into the team's way of working because of lack of attention, forgetfulness, or laziness. Don't be disappointed, but don't ignore this—be deliberate about reminding people and keeping them alert to their promises.

Phase 5. Identity Shifts and Rubber Hits the Road

A People are willing to make change, but still need direction

Tools
- Finding Your Place
- Givens and Challenges
- Dynamic Plenaries
- Updating Our Identity
- Bringing It Home Video

Evidence of completion?
Leadership community organizes on behalf of the organization

A shared sense of momentum

The challenge
For Leader:
What must we get to grips with?

For Community:
Is this too big for us?

Focus questions
What are the few big challenges?
How do we build courage to face up to them?

Sign of progress?
- Leaders face dilemmas and commit to action
- Individuals find ways to be productive

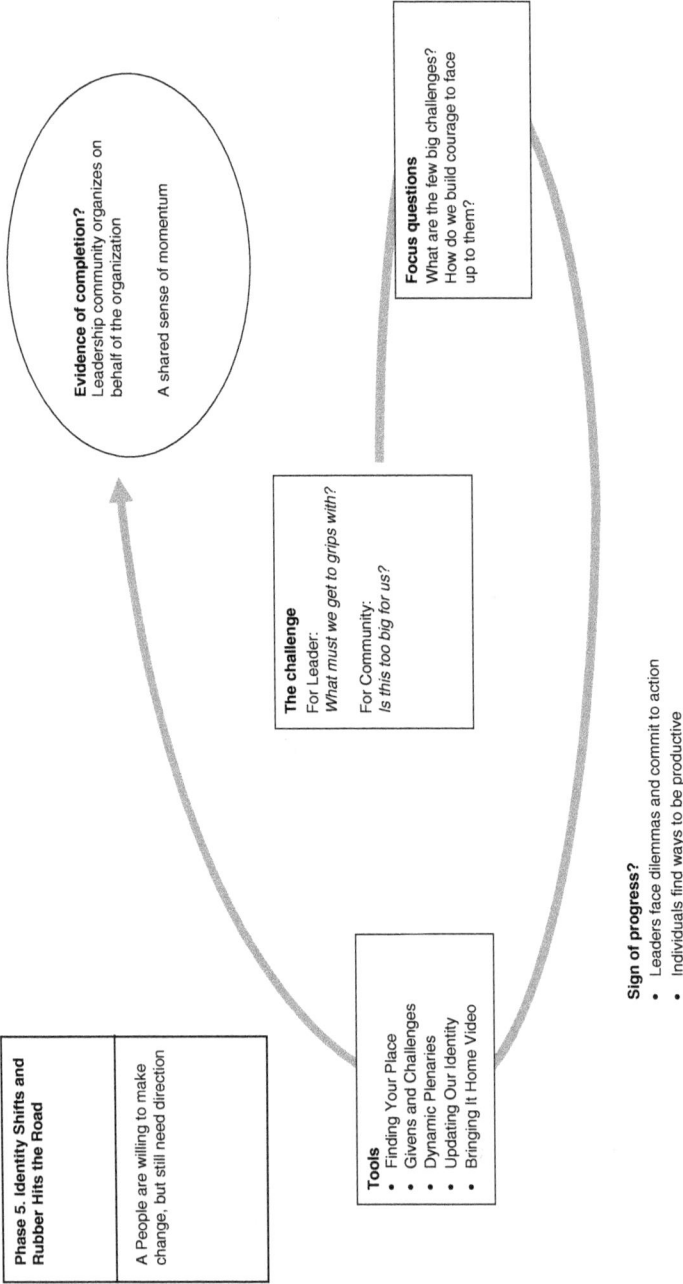

Figure 7.1 Phase 5 summary

PART 3

The Path

Herd of gazelles prancing

CHAPTER 8

Harnessing Passion and Purpose in a Compelling Story of Alignment

Following the Dar meeting we entered the third year as a new region, during which the regional team saw its postmerger improvement in results reaching new heights:

- A threefold increase in the customer base
- An 80 percent increase in the income across all three major business areas
- A 10 percent reduction in its cost base.

The extent of these improvements was unprecedented in any of our constituent countries, and it was evident that the decision to create the new region and the method for doing so were paying off handsomely. We wanted to be able to replicate this success in the future, with other own teams in other regions and in entirely different organizations, so we made it our next task to describe as precisely as we could what had made the difference.

As you will recall, Philip had embarked on the merger by bringing together the new leadership team in Nairobi, and he gathered the team physically on four more occasions after Nairobi up to and including Dar, at roughly 6-month intervals. While most people would agree that one such meeting is necessary to get the ball rolling, this was a far larger investment in management time and consultancy fees (not to mention air fares and hotel accommodation), demanding from everyone involved a sustained commitment over time. It is widely known that leadership team get-togethers don't always justify the cost, and we wanted to pinpoint what in particular had occurred in this case to repay the investment.

That is why we approached several senior managers in the regional leadership team. Mark, one of the most experienced country directors, was in no doubt about the approach taken:

> It benefits all our target audiences—and as employees we have more belief in ourselves. Our customers understand what we're doing and why we're doing it. We have a newer and simpler narrative, which is about "creating opportunities for young people and modernizing UK–African relationships." It's easier to communicate and more satisfying to do . . . although there's still a hell of a long way to go.

Mark's passion and purpose were evident in those remarks, but we were struck by one word he used, "narrative." We had introduced a narrative method at the Dar meeting when we feared that the evident enthusiasm of the 30 leaders might soon dissipate. So we asked small groups to put together their own brief accounts of the merger. One group told us that it began with everyone behaving like hippos, defensive and willing to be aggressive too. This was memorable.

Then we asked three subgroups to focus on before, during, and after, and each to provide a sentence or two that when taken together provided this whole team version:

> Before: *When we started two years ago, we were East and West, separate countries, separate regions, possessive, parochial, suspicious, and not wanting to share. The new East and West Africa region was all hot air and nothing real.*
>
> During: *There were lots of things needing to be challenged and done in order to create a sustainable platform from which to develop regional products that customers valued and staff believed in.*
>
> *Each of our leadership meetings raised difficult questions, created challenging situations, and uncovered precious moments that helped bring us through to where we are now. In particular, Lagos taught us about leadership, leadership, leadership and how despite*

*the tension that comes from change you can still engage and ener-
gize everyone, despite all the difficulties of geography and numbers.
After: Now, as decision makers for the region we are creating success, reputation, and enjoyment. We are not afraid of challenges or diversity.*

Many people told us their personal story, and their enthusiasm con-
veyed a solid belief in the new region and their place in it. For example,
Akello told us how her country built on another's success in delivering a
new regional product:

One of the countries started off in a really interesting way. They
had gone to the radio and TV stations and succeeded in getting
thousands of young people excited and talking about development
goals to the whole country. It was very inspiring and I talked with
my colleagues there to find out how they managed to reach such
large numbers. We then took up the same initiative in our country.
It was very easy because we weren't reinventing the wheel. We also
learned from another country about getting through to the youth
ministry and getting access on the ground and we copied that too.

In that example Akello and her colleagues are copying what worked
and drawing in new ways of working from another country. The new
regional product she is describing is one of a handful of blockbuster products designed in the region to replace the myriad of diverse single-country
initiatives in order to raise the relevance, reputation, and impact of the
East and West Africa region with its customers. By year 3, those new
regional products were being delivered across multiple countries and producing the dramatic expansion in customer base and income. As each
country reported its improving results, they attracted the attention of
others who saw the benefits in adopting the new regional products. In
this way, the change program gathered pace and momentum: The new
products enabled the results and the changes in working methods. Everything was inextricably linked.

With their results improving, the teams we brought together from
across the region became more confident to share their *back home* realities,
facing up to and grappling with all sorts of vulnerabilities and challenges

they had in common. Individuals who previously confided in a narrow circle of in-country colleagues were expanding their communication and contributing to a growing pool of ideas and inspiration being accessed by all 11 countries in the new region. The additive effect was sparking off a solution-led culture with a *can-do* attitude.

Here are some more examples of how the individuals began to feel and act differently:

- *Fatima* who made a stand for local staff being heard in the very first meeting had her eyes opened as a result and changed her vision of how to work in the organization.
- *Binte* who was shocked when first asked to attend the workshop was later on asking herself, "Is this really me standing in front of colleagues providing them with knowledge?"
- *Ian* shrugged his shoulders at first but then made brave early moves in a small influential group and set new things in motion.
- *Yahya* who earlier was adamant that in Africa pecking order and strong hierarchical leadership were important, later recognized how a leader must also be supportive, making people creative and carrying everyone along.
- *Akello* at first unable to see how a big region could benefit her small provincial office, later felt empowered to take on a regional responsibility bringing people from 15 other countries, reaching out even beyond the new region, to progress a major project she was leading.
- *Otim* unsure of what to make of regionalization, took on a role of communicating changes to staff and then became a confident team leader of country directors charged with finding new sources of income.
- *Foluke* who at first appeared quiet and shy, then found her voice while giving clear and objective feedback to the leadership team on some highly contentious staff issues, which in turn, propelled a deeper shift in attitudes and behavior.
- For *Gail*, frustrated and unable to get heard or understood in a leadership team dominated by men, the gender issue completely went away. She transformed her country office from dark, dingy, and down in the dumps to one that delivers and is now at the forefront of regional innovation.

- *Gabriel* coming in half way through the film caught the change bug, and once enthused he set off to tackle some long-standing performance issues, liberating his office from the shackles of the past and creating an overwhelmingly positive *can-do* attitude among his team members.
- *Mark* who admitted to initial cynicism, based on difficult previous experiences of regionalization, became a convert, recognized for his creative talent and became a leading light in taking the region's new agenda forward.

Passionate stories from the 30 leaders were testament to how they were changing themselves and sparking change in others around them. Evidently an alignment was occurring between them all, but how? This caused us to reflect.

When you stop to think about alignment, it has an inner and outer aspect. We said inner alignment is when one person's head, heart, and hand are *at one,* and then a person's full creative energy is available to them, the evidence being manifest in their increasing confidence and influence. To become a high-performing team, senior managers have first to transform themselves. This alignment happens through reflection and a change of heart, in other words, a kind of personal change. Gabriel, a country director, described it well:

> The thing that we're talking about here is not just change-about-them, but it's a change-about-us.

The outer aspect of alignment occurs when committed colleagues and team members come together and combine their energies to multiply their total impact. Their work to align begins naturally when they clarify together where they are right now and what they actually know, and then their work advances in small, agreed, and doable steps. When they are called to account for progress at their next gathering, the team members can grow in confidence through sharing their successes and learning from their shortfalls. This alignment requires time, dedication, and a constancy of commitment, and we have looked for ways to speed this up by getting down to the essentials and dispensing with the rest.

Inspired by Francisco Varela (Maturana and Varela, 1988) we found it helpful to think of the merged East and West Africa region as an *organism* in an *ecosystem*. Our newly born *organism* was represented by 30 leaders drawn from 11 different countries, and their work was to forge their unique team character and identity. Each time we brought that team back together, instead of jumping straight into a busy agenda, we allowed time to *re-member* the team identity, as if we were waking a slumbering giant. We began by dividing the 30 members into pairs to post their responses to questions such as "What are we, as the regional team, seeking to achieve?" "What progress have we made since last time?" "What have we learned?" "What challenges and opportunities do we see today?" The flipcharts containing their responses added up to the story of the team, and we played it back to them as confirmation of who they were. This first hour at the beginning of each 3-day meeting made everyone—whether they were new or established in this team—purposeful and active. Then we charged them jointly with writing the next chapter in their story. We were consciously challenging the hippos, refusing to tolerate their violence while encouraging the shy ones out of passivity and bringing all team members to align, for strength, speed, and adaptability, like a herd of gazelles, fit and ready for the difficult topics they had to face up to.

This groundwork, over the series, created the conditions for a certain magic to take place, but it was a long time coming. The magic moments arrived all of a sudden as if the minds all went *click* simultaneously, and the individuals took on a new team identity. One was in phase three in Addis, when the 30 leaders realized that they were all in the same boat, and then it made sense for them to unite in the face of adversity. This was their *urge to merge*. The magic happened again, but differently, in phase five in Dar es Salaam when the 30 leaders realized that they were being trusted by the wider organization of 500 to be the decision makers.

Through 500 staff taking on the new products and changing their ways of working, the key customer relationships in each country were improved and so were the results. Many people across the region enjoyed the benefits, and Binte's example of one member of staff being given greater responsibility is illustrative:

A colleague who has worked in the library for years finds out the library is closing threatening his job. He is afraid that he doesn't have the capacity to deliver new products because that is exposing him to a wider context he doesn't know. He is asking himself "do I have the skills to meet the challenge?" But when he is actually selected for the role of project manager for the pan-African schools project, it is like a promotion: He is coordinating a regional program, linking with colleagues in other countries. It boosts his capacity!

It wasn't simply magic though, because considerable effort was required in each county to make their change into a positive experience. Gail was newly promoted when she was posted to a different country and placed in charge of a poor-performing office. At the same time she joined the regional leadership team where she was able to tap into the experience of a colleague who helped her carry forward the change in her country. This is what they did:

We started having gentle but honest conversations with staff, communicating the region's strategy early on, including evidence of what we're good at and what we need to work on. We got teams working on the gaps, so by the time I announced the structure none of it was news to them! We let people choose openly between voluntary redundancy or applying for jobs in the new structure alongside external applicants. Quite a few we wanted to retain opted to go, and obviously we had people who wanted to stay and didn't get jobs, but I think their transition was well managed too. We even held a party to celebrate the past success and to mark the end of an era. Some people who were leaving said "thank you" to me. We now have a team in place who are able to deliver.

The dignity offered to everyone in Gail's example is one of the conditions provided in every country across the East and West Africa region that helped the whole change keep moving forward instead of running out of steam. We saw a whole community becoming like leaders, accustomed to tackling deeply difficult dilemmas, taking concrete actions, and keeping their colleagues onboard. They were learning to work successfully with conflict both in the group and more widely. Instead of so-called change fatigue, they found it easier and easier to identify and solve new challenges as soon as these arrived. All in all, the people in this region were becoming quite special.

We are reluctant to use the word transformation because it sounds so grand and permanent, but we were seeing an effect amplified, and Philip and his regional team worked to embed the gains in several practical ways (as observed below by staff members), including communication:

> Philip sends a monthly newsletter and there are bulletins to all staff so you know what is expected and nothing comes as a surprise. It tells people what has been going on, what we are still doing, what has been going well, what the challenges are, how we need to improve ourselves . . . so that keeps you on your toes of what is really happening

. . . harmonized terms and conditions, through a single regional pay and grade structure:

> The terms and conditions have varied but now we have new terms and conditions that staff appreciates very much. We no longer say "my country is different, the East is different from the West." A lot of issues have been synchronized and that has helped with staff morale.

. . . a recognition scheme:

> They introduced a scheme, really looking through at what people do and giving you the chance to nominate yourself, a colleague, or a group that performed particularly well, especially in the drive toward our strategic plan. This comes with a small financial reward; then on top of that, there is the noticing and the naming: It is copied to everyone in the region, so everyone knows. This encourages people to do things and to notice when they feel their colleagues are doing their best. It makes people feel proud, and also to remember I need to get my act together.

. . . and a comprehensive training program with self-study modules supported by trained coaches.

Foluke, one of our African senior managers, describes it like this:

> Changes come and go and often an organization reverts to established behavior patterns. This change program took it to the next level . . . This was change that has made a difference.

While the improvement in business results is something we are proud of, the positive change in individuals and in the team as a whole to keep meeting each new challenge as it arrived is the more remarkable part of the story and such an amazing tribute to the ability of people to expand their contribution when they have the right conditions.

A *can do* ethos was evident in staff across the entire region and, to capture how this was brought about, we summarized the steps in a *path to alignment* (overleaf) that we offer to those of you with a similar ambition. You can see this summary in Table 8.1.

Table 8.1 The path to alignment across an organization (summary of five phases)

Phase and action	The challenge	Focus questions	Signs of progress	Tools	Evidence of completion
1. **Looming danger and making the first call.** The leader alerts the leadership community.	For leader: *How do I deliver this message?* For community: *How can I get through this without changing?*	Where are we now? What does the future look like? What are the first steps?	• The leader is motivating not frightening people. • The challenge is clearly and explicitly framed.	• Six Thinking Hats • Visioning 5/1/3 • Transition Planning • Five-Min Process Review	• Leadership community united in inaction, trying to maintain the status quo. • Leader thwarted or tricked into believing others are engaged.
2. **Lame response and making the second call.** The call is ignored, the leader pushes harder.	For leader: *How do I wake them up?* For community: *Why is the leader being so stupid and nasty?*	What's new? How do we recover control? What do we keep/ let go of?	• People are exposed to new attitudes and behaviors. • Resistance is recognized and explored. • 75% know change is necessary.	• Stakeholder Contact • Three Circles • The Mirror • Timeline	• Leadership community stepped from the past into the future, but may feel sad and lost. • Leader may be angry, at the group's resistance.
3. **Leadership community aligns and steps up.** The community falls apart then regroups.	For leader: *How do I transfer ownership?* For community: *How can I influence?*	What do I know? What do you know? How do we take decisions?	• People grapple with how to change. • Members unite. • Individuals find an action they are passionate to implement.	• Thing of Beauty • Steering Group • Social Mapping and Swarms	• Leadership community are bonded, engaged, and confident. "We know what we need to do." • Leader feels relief and progress.

4. People pull back . . . then accept the new reality. The leadership community takes the change back home.	For leader: *How do we engage the wider team?* For community: *Now I'm enthusiastic; why is my team not?*	What do you want from me? What do I want from you?	• Staff share both +/- stories. • Difficult issues are out on the table. • Leaders commit to simple actions and behaviors.	• Staff Research • Rackets • Stories—Talking in the Round • Action Plans	• Staff speak up on issues that concern them. • Leadership community recognizes how their behavior contributes. • All "in the same boat."
5. Identity shifts and rubber hits the road. People are willing to make change but still need direction.	For leader: *What must we get to grips with?* For community: *Is this too big for us? . . .*	What are the few big challenges? How do we build courage to face up to them?	• Leaders face dilemmas and commit to action. • Individuals find ways to be productive.	• Finding Your Place • Givens and Challenges • Dynamic Plenaries • Updating Our Identity • Bringing It Home Video	• Leadership community organizes on behalf of the organization. • A shared sense of momentum.

CHAPTER 9

Choosing Your Path and Bringing Others With You

We believed that creating the *can do* ethos across the new region was a most notable achievement. But the first time this was put to the test we were wrong-footed and our account was unconvincing. We needed an overarching and better-argued rationale for why leaders must create leadership, and we wanted to confront leaders with a clear choice, spelling out any likely consequences. It happened like this.

Ten years ago, Tony was summoned unexpectedly to a meeting with the global head of human resources in the London headquarters of Philip's organization where, over a cup of coffee, he was shown page upon page of bar charts and numeric tables and asked to explain the East and West Africa's annual staff survey results, compared with those from the 12 other regions and the 112 country operations spanning the globe. Sub-Saharan Africa was widely regarded as a no-hoper because it traditionally scored low, and recent scores had sometimes dipped further. But the region's latest results, measured 3 years after the merger, were standing out starkly and required explanation because they had risen so spectacularly to the very top of the company tables, with a 74 percent score for *confidence in the leadership* beating the norm for the best UK organizations (top 10 public and private sector organizations in the United Kingdom measured by Ipsos MORI). And the region's results for *leadership of change* were twice as positive as those top 10 organizations.

Delighted to discover this, but also caught unexpectedly by the request for an explanation, Tony described with a growing sense of excitement the five meetings in Africa that produced a wave of change rippling across Philip's entire organization and illustrated this with a rough diagram (similar to Figure 2.1). He said that it was an unusual change program because it opened people's hearts and minds, producing a *can do* attitude that released everyone from the cycle of poor performance and dependency that bogged them down. Nonplussed and slightly baffled, the head of HR asked, "But why did this change program deliver when so few do?" Tony could only recap, but failed to provide the head of HR with the exact form of illumination he required.

After that peculiar meeting Tony reported back to Philip, and we worked out how to set out our stall properly. We produced the fable to convey the essentials in a language that we hoped everyone of whatever age or background could understand. And we also arrived at a fuller explanation of the choices faced by a leader, which will bring this to a close.

We would like to invite you to reflect on your role as a leader in the context surrounding you. On the *Titanic* the captain presumed to know more than those in the engine room, with a disastrous result. When leaders are more democratic or more laissez-faire the results can be equally disastrous. During complex, large-scale change, not only must we overturn the notion that the leader has all the answers, but also a second notion that the leader has the right questions! We believe that the leader has to continue making sure results are produced while constantly finding out and responding to the unasked questions, despite those questions becoming quite negative, such as, "Why is the leader being so stupid and nasty?" "How can I get through this without changing?"

Many leaders asked to merge organizations begin with restructuring, but as soon as this threatens people's jobs, the changes in attitudes, behaviors, and ways of working they aimed to bring about will come to a rapid halt. Yet a tiny amount of empathy shows that a librarian will grieve for the closure of an expensive resource center they have given birth to and a teacher will be bereft when their poorly performing teaching center is shut, just like the coal miner whose pit is closed and the shipbuilder who for economic and political reasons is no longer required to work. Any change imposed from on high naturally produces sadness and anger and disengagement, not only among those who leave, but also among those who remain. The approach that imposes change creates losers not leaders, and the hidden costs are huge but incalculable. So it is a great mystery to us why so much technical expertise, money, and other resources are so often invested in change programs that produce such poor results.

If you are leading a poorly performing organization, and you choose to reduce costs by imposing cuts, our experience with poorly performing organizations in a depressed region show you will deepen the malaise. A Nobel Prize winning economist, Douglass C. North (2005), hit the nail on the head when he described "institutional rigidities" made up of unwritten rules, assumptions, beliefs, and behaviors that become a huge barrier, whether to results in a single organization or to wider economic and social progress across entire countries, most notably in the poorest places on earth such as Cameroon, where year after year things fail to improve.

We believe it is foolish to ignore the institutional rigidities that Douglass North described. From our experience with a complex organization dispersed in 11 small offices across a vast region, it was essential to orchestrate growth, because simply to impose cuts would drive those operations into the sand, dampening or killing their impact, relevance, and viability.

That is why we set out with a different approach, and we saw results continuing to improve day in and day out, year in year out in the East and West Africa region. Remarkably, the rising trend was not dented by several necessary restructurings faced by more than half the people in this region, and the reason was those restructurings were owned and chosen close to home, rather than imposed remotely. We had mobilized people in the new region to face up to the real challenges themselves, of relevance, cost, and viability, instead of waiting for an axe to fall. They came to recognize that they did not have the luxury of waiting for a magical solution. Our part in this as leaders was to bring people together, share the performance information, discuss the realities of investment and impact, and invite them to create ways of scaling up their results and to take any tough decisions needed, thus make themselves leaders not losers.

This articulated why and how the *can-do* attitude was produced and, as we have shown, the bottom-line benefits were enormous.

Now let us go back to the start. We began Chapter 1 with a question about leadership: "How do we create the adaptable organization thriving in the face of an uncertain and rapidly changing world?" We have described what we learned about 10 years ago creating leadership for change, and today as we look around us, the key features of uncertainty—connectedness, scale, pace, and information—that shaped our approach have only intensified. The banking collapse, global insecurity, refugee crises, and economic nationalism are headline examples of such uncertainty. Each of those events creates a new operational context for organizations, and like storm waves on the beach, they keep on rolling in, while their rate of arrival seems to be increasing.

Part of our story was about the power of numbers where one leader engages 30, who in turn engage 500, to create an organization relevant, aligned in purpose across 11 different country offices, and capable of delivering at scale. But the story was not only about numbers, because 500 people unlocked for one another a new reality within which greater results were possible. Gail's words illustrate how this new reality looked and felt to people at a country level:

> There's a story to be told of an office that was once run on very hierarchical lines with a very unclear program seen as a sort of donor agency because that was the interest of the people working here. It is a journey the team has taken from stopping all of that and getting into being much more outward focused with some very dynamic staff, all of whom are locally appointed. We listen to our customers, have more fun, and are much more creative and involved. Our voice is now being heard in the region. We've got a big old colonial building that before was small rooms, dark, and dingy and now we've opened up the space, got great colors everywhere and it's a different place! Now we're seen as a country that delivers!

When we examined many such examples in East and West Africa, we found that the staff, who used to behave like sleepy villagers and angry hippos, were liberated, as if by a magic wand, into fast-moving and adaptive gazelles. So we looked carefully for what had produced this transformation. In each case a country director worked closely with their team to release everyone from a current reality that no one really enjoyed *(what is)*, into a new setting more closely aligned to the organizational purpose *(what can be)*. The change that was visceral and inside the skin of each team member, soon became visible to outsiders.

But we are inviting you and your organization to begin with realism, by choosing to see the world as it is, rather than how you wish it to be. When you pretend the world is easy to understand, you create a false security for your organization and, in doing so, you fail your people by encouraging their immobility. If instead everyone can recognize the world is complex and constantly shifting—full of unknowns—you are giving them the opportunity to adapt and starting to build the readiness throughout the organization to manage the true uncertainty.

We are suggesting that you invite people to adapt, letting them illuminate and get to grips with the very real challenges they face. When we did so the advances took time. It took real commitment and there were setbacks along the way. But the changes were substantial and lasting within the organization, not only because they were accepted by its people, but because those people invented the changes themselves, as if they were the leaders. In effect we were spreading and dispersing the leadership.

We have since distilled five principles that contain the essence we carry forward into our work of creating leaders. We are pleased to share these with you.

1. *The leader has a clear message, without all the answers . . . nor do they have all the right questions!* At times you might feel a great certainty that tempts you to say and do far more than is good for everyone: perhaps to show off your knowledge. When you push people hard with actions you believe will revolutionize the organization, beware the hippos who will fight and bite and turn you into another one just like them, fighting in the mud! But look out for the quiet people who unless actively called on to contribute will stay silent or drift away. Take care to give the clear message that helps people, who are bombarded with information, focus on a few important things to pay attention to, and set the framework in which the right questions and answers emerge, producing purposeful action to deliver the solutions. Remember the African proverb "One head does not contain all the wisdom."

2. *The leader's behavior rings bells.* When you say something but do nothing, your powerlessness infects the organization. When you say one thing and do another, you provoke cynicism and it spreads. Remember to reinforce your message through your stories, your decisions, and your behavior. It is energizing for the team to see

through your concrete actions that you mean what you say and that you walk the talk. If you remind your team about what you said you would do and regularly update them on progress, they gain a sense of purpose and momentum. And when it doesn't go so well, they will appreciate your honesty and want to tell you the truth too. As trust grows between you, they will want to listen more. Such simple, visible changes in your behavior can reinforce your message, make lights flash, bells ring, whistles blow! Why not grab and inspire people like this, rather than just telling them what to do?

3. *The Leader calls . . . and responds.* When you want something from your team, you don't keep it to yourself: You make the call. But what do you do in the moments that follow? You can repeat the call and say it louder with more urgency or you can slow down, listening carefully and responding directly to what comes back. As a leader you are willing to wait and listen for the reply and take the time to ponder because your aim is not only to influence but also to be influenced. With care and purpose, you are creating a dialogue like the call and response within a musical improvisation—sometimes surprising, sometimes beautiful, sometimes unnerving—but building with increasing understanding, on each note that was played so far. That to-and-fro reminds us of a pattern you notice between dancers as they take on each other's moves, and in African drumming where the rhythm of one drum both echoes and continues on from another. Through consciously building up the interplays between *leader* and *follower* you are gaining control of the pace, not by speaking faster or pushing on more urgently into action, but by slowing down and responding more directly to the people who need to be engaged. Together you are building up the muscles and forming the new habits to share the information, integrate, learn, and adapt. So listen carefully to others, and listen to yourself.

4. *The leader steps back to create space.* A leader often pushes too fast for results. Remember, when the young chief shook his stick the other chiefs just resisted him, by getting angry or falling asleep. When you are tempted to toughen up and demand more, ask yourself what you really want. Do you want to knock the team off balance and push them into a corner? Do you want team members to close up and

block? Or do you want the individuals to start behaving like leaders, sharing what they know with each other, integrating it quickly, creating new possibilities, and influencing one another's decisions. If you want to nurture a team's shared understanding and a journey of engagement, you will soften, step back, and listen and draw the team into the leadership space. Good facilitation helps by bringing people in or out of the spotlight, drawing them forward or backward, to counter their habit of passivity or dominance, and showing them moves that can be copied across an entire organization. As they learn to occupy and share the space you offer, you may notice their eyes begin to sparkle.

5. *The leader uses the head, the hands, and the heart.* A leader balances the three agendas of thinking, doing, and feeling, allowing their head, hands, and heart to work in harmony, like a healthy human being. You might need to begin with thinking, to offer the rationale that everyone is demanding. Then the doing might become urgent: drawing up plans, allocating tasks and resources. But don't forget the heart, as many leaders do, because you only store up difficulties. If you give time and importance to the feelings of the team, including your own, the hearts will soon move, to replace the insecurity and negativity that change always produces with trust, courage, and passion. By including all three agendas and bringing forward the one required in each phase and at each moment, you will find it much easier to land your messages, to adjust your behavior and ring bells, to call and respond, and to create the space that draw others into leadership. The three agendas build up the team's muscle, providing everyone with the *why,* the *what,* and the *how* that equips them to lead.

What these five principles recognize is that people are the best agents of change. In the process of creating alignment, the leader is supporting everyone to be agents of change and the creators of an adaptive organization.

In the years since this change story in Africa, we have continued to explore the second path, which leads your organization into adaptation, and why it is a better choice than the first path of defensiveness.

Our further experience with leaders and teams, in various organizations and geographies, has produced a few final tips for creating and dispersing the leadership.

Dispersed leadership is not applicable for every leader in every situation. Leaders ask us, "How does dispersed leadership work in an emergency?" We have seen amazing responses to crises, natural disasters, accidents, and emergencies, and we are in no doubt that directional leadership gives the quickest and best response. During the period of the emergency, your ambitions to disperse the leadership must fall into the background: You follow strict protocols and processes that your organization carefully drew up, tested, and put into place for exactly these circumstances. But what happens during the crisis to the business that must be kept running? Here your earlier investment in dispersing the leadership pays off because the leaders throughout your organization could not have been better prepared to take up responsibility.

Dispersed leadership takes time. Leaders tell us, "My heart says you're right, but I don't have time to implement this, because I have a board and shareholders to satisfy." Of course people take time to trust, after all you are asking them to operate differently and to work with colleagues in a completely new way. Our imperfect world is impatient. Results can never wait until tomorrow: Without delivering performance today Philip would have destroyed credibility with his stakeholders, and we expect that is also true for you. He managed by delivering performance gains early, to build up everyone's confidence to go after sustainable performance gains further down the line. Like Philip, you will need results now as well as tomorrow, and to get this you have to adapt your style, both pushing for performance today while also drawing your people into leadership to create greater performance tomorrow.

Long after our first meeting in London, we came to realize that the leader was creating the three conditions of *willingness, capacity, and confidence* to allow everyone to step together into the unknown and that these three conditions were key to delivering each successful change journey.

Creating a real *willingness* to step into the leadership is never easy. Everyone has a tendency to hold onto the past—whether it works for them or not—simply because it is familiar. People will tell you, "Well, this is how we work around here" not only with pride, but often disdain.

Negative experiences make them cynical, skeptical, or reluctant to try anything different. A willingness to change is often pretended without really meaning it. Your three essential steps as a leader to create willingness are as follows:

- Loosen people's grip with the past—acknowledge the past but get them ready to let it go;
- Help teams see the reality of the challenge they face through clarification and reclarification;
- Create the space for your team to dream of what they can do and who they can be.

Building *capacity* to be leaders is not only a matter of training but also a matter of reflection and learning in a team. When you bring a leadership team together, many will expect to produce an action plan, and if you tell them "We do not mind what you decide here in this meeting because we are building your ability to take effective decisions and actions in between these meetings," at first they might be confused. But to build the capacity of leaders, you all need to practice new habits and behaviors together: reflection, challenge, learning, and coordinated action in response to evidence. You will find yourself exploring how decisions will be made and what kind of freedom and accountability will be provided. You need to build trust to a much higher level before the team will respond quickly enough to the pace of the outside world. Each leader and team needs to ask themselves truthfully, How are we contributing personally and collectively to creating this status quo? What shifts are we willing to make to be different? Through such questions you are building capacity.

Building *confidence* is done both individually and collectively. When people talk about their organizations in negative tones as they often do ("Agh, that's just what we're like") notice how they are telling a story that lets everyone off the hook. Each time they repeat such a story about their own team or organization they are making a choice, perhaps unconsciously, to continue performing badly. This blocks others from disturbing them and ducks their responsibility to change. Breaking such a bad habit can be hard, but you can begin as we do, by agreeing just a couple of modest, short-term doable actions, and recording the small successes.

You can have leaders stop, look back, and recognize what they've done. Write it down. Share it on social media. Any achievement capture can build confidence to bite off slightly more and this can be nurtured into a *can do* mentality. They will start to say, "If we tackled challenge X, then why can't we tackle challenge Y." It puts something in their gas tank for when things don't go well: "This may not have worked, but this is what we learned." You can soon point to examples when what appeared a failure actually became the starting point for their next success.

We have brought you to a fork in the road, where the first path is for the leaders who lay out all the answers and steps for everyone to follow. Those leaders seek to provide organizational security through the certainty of process, structure, and plan. But we showed that ultimately this can only produce success if the world remains constant. It brushes aside the question *What if?*

This book describes the second path that is chosen by leaders who recognize that, despite their best-laid plans, the world does not unfold as they wish it to. You take this path when you want your organization to thrive in the face of complexity and uncertainty. You seek to create conditions in which the organization gets smarter and faster, harnessing the collective wisdom of its *leader–followers* to learn and adapt and to do so at speed. You are building everyone's resilience because there is one certainty: The world is going to change, and quickly, and probably unexpectedly. Your job as a leader is to place everyone in a position to respond to that certainty. That is why you are creating leaders and dispersing the leadership.

So here we are. Being a leader on the second path means that you will bring people together on a journey requiring new habits that will in due course come to define who they are. This journey can feel like a mountain to climb, with every peak you reach only bringing you to yet another peak beyond, but isn't this preferable to the defensive leadership that buries your heads in the sand?

We've described the benefit of looking backward as well as forward, and we believe this practice is at the heart of the matter. It gives you (and your team) the energy to continue. You will gain as much from the wonder of where you've been and the terrain you've already covered, as from the excitement of where you're going next. We can promise that this brings real pleasure to a team, inspiring them to seek out the new peaks to be climbed because they are fuelled by where they've already been.

We invite you to keep looking up and down the mountain and enjoying the view because this kind of leadership offers everyone the greater resilience and courage they will need to tackle the unknown challenges ahead.

The End

Bibliography

Bennis, W. (2000). *Intelligent Leadership—Creating a Passion for Change* (p. vii). New York City, NY: Random House Business Books.

Bieshaar, H., J. Knight, and A. van Wassenaer. (2001). Deals that create value. *McKinsey Quarterly* 1, pp. 64–73.

Bohm, D. (1990). *On Dialogue*. Cambridge, UK: Pegasus.

Bourque, N., and G. Johnson. (2008). "Strategy Workshops and 'Awaydays' as Ritual." In *The Oxford Handbook of Organizational Decision Making,* eds. G. Hodgkinson, and W. Starbuck. Oxford, UK: Oxford University Press.

Bowlby, J. (1951). *Child Care and the Growth of Love*. Harmondsworth, UK: Penguin.

Bresnitz, S. (1989). Enhancing Performance Under Stress by Information About Its Expected Duration. Final Report. NTIS.

Bridges, W. (1980*). Transitions—Making Sense of Life's Chang*es. Boston, MA: Nicholas Brealey.

Cooperrider, D., and D. Whitney. (2005). *Appreciative Inquiry—A Positive Revolution in Change*. Oakland, CA*:* Berrett-Koehler.

Covey, S. (1989). *The Seven Habits of Highly Effective People*. New York, NY: Simon and Schuster.

De Bono, E. (2000). *Six Thinking Hats*. Westminster, UK: Penguin.

Denning, S. (2004). Telling tales. *Harvard Business Review*. Reprint.

Festinger, L. (1957). *A Theory of Cognitive Dissonance*. Stanford, CA: Stanford University.

Fiske, P. (2007). *Learning to Listen*. British Council. (A policy paper on Intercultural dialogue.)

Goleman, D. (2003). *Destructive Emotions* (p. 306). London, UK: Bloomsbury.

Goodwin, P. (November, 2009). "Spanning boundaries: Social Innovation in a Complex World." In *Transforming Innovation to Address Social Challenges, Committee for Scientific and Technological Policy* (pp. 59–64). Paris, France: OECD.

Goodwin, P., and T. Page. (2011). *Leading Strategy as a Journey of Not Knowing*. www.pageconsulting.co.uk.

Greaves, N. (1988). *When Hippo Was Hairy*. Bok Books.

Hampden-Turner, C. (1990). *Charting the Corporate Mind—From Dilemma to Strategy*. Hoboken, NJ: Wiley Blackwell.

Handy, C. (2008). *Myself and Other More Important Matters*. New York, NY: Amacom.

Hellinger, B., and G. Ten Heovel. (1999) *Acknowledging What Is: Conversations with Bert Hellinger*. Phoenix, AZ: Zeig, Tucker & Co.

Hirschhorn, L. (1999). "The primary risk." *Human Relations* 52, no. 1, pp. 5–23.

Isaacs, W. (1999). *Dialogue and the Art of Thinking Together*. New York, NY: Currency.

Kotter, J.P. (1995). Leading change—why transformation efforts fail. *Harvard Business Review*.

Kotter, J., and D. Cohen. (2002). *The Heart of Change*. Boston, MA: Harvard Business School.

Kubler-Ross, E. (1973). *On Death and Dying*. London, UK: Routledge.

Lewin, K. (1997). *Resolving Social Conflicts and Field Theory in Social Science*. Washington, D.C: American Psychological Association.

Losada, M., and E. Heaphy. (2004). "The role of positivity and connectivity in the performance of business teams: A nonlinear dynamics model." *American Behavioral Scientist* 47, no. 6, pp. 740–765.

Marlier, D., and C. Parker. (2009). *Engaging Leadership—Three Agendas for Sustaining Achievement*. Basingstoke, UK: Palgrave Macmillan.

Maturana, H., and F. Varela. (1988). *The Tree of Knowledge—The Biological Roots of Human Understanding*. Boulder, CO: Shambhala.

Mindell, A. (1992). *The Leader as Martial Artist*. New York, NY: Harper.

North, D.C. (2005). *Understanding the Process of Economic Change*. New York, NY: Princeton.

Oshry, B. (1996). *Seeing Systems—Unlocking the Mysteries of Organisational Life*. Oakland, CA: Berrett-Koehler.

Owen, H. (1997). *Open Space Technology—A User's Guide*. Oakland, CA: Berrett-Koehler.

Page, T. (1996). *Diary of a Change Agent*. Farnham, UK: Gower.

Page, T. (2008). "Writing stories to facilitate an African merger." *Organisations & People* 15, no. 1, pp. 56–61.

Page, T., and C. Vascotto. (2011). "Adapting awayday rituals to deliver in difficult times." *Organisations and People* 18, no. 1, pp. 74–83.

Pascale, R., T. Goss, and A. Athos. (1993). "The reinvention roller coaster—risking the present for a powerful future." *Harvard Business Review*.

Prochaska, J., D. Levesque, and J. Prochaska. (2001). "Mastering change—A core competency for employees." *Brief Treatment and Crisis Intervention* 1, no. 1, pp. 7–15.

Schutz, W. (1994). *The Human Element—Productivity, Self-esteem and the Bottom Line*. Hoboken, NJ: Jossey Bass.

Sirkin, H., P. Keenan, and A. Jackson. (2005). "The hard side of change management." *Harvard Business Review*.

Spillane, J.P. (2006). *Distributed Leadership*. Hoboken, NJ: Jossey Bass.

Torbert, B. (2004). *Action Inquiry—The Secret of Timely and Transforming Leadership*. Oakland, CA: Berrett-Koehler.

Weisbord, M.R., and S. Janoff. (1995). *Future Search—An Action Guide to Finding Common Ground in Organisations and Communities*. Oakland, CA: Berrett-Koehler.

Wheatley, M. (1994). *Leadership and the New Science*. Oakland, CA: Berrett-Koehler.

About the Authors

Philip Goodwin has been a CEO in the international development sector for over seven years. He was previously a senior executive with British Council, the UK cultural relations organization, and has lived and worked in numerous countries around the world. He holds a doctorate in cultural geography from the University of London.

Tony Page is a UK-based facilitator whose career has taken him to Europe, Africa, the Asia–Pacific, and the Americans to work with leaders and teams in government agencies, NGOs, and corporates. He is the author of *Diary of a Change Agent* (Page, 1996) and numerous published articles that describe a narrative approach to change. A chartered occupational psychologist, he graduated from Nottingham University. Nowadays he continues to write and to offer his consultancy services as a volunteer.

Index

OTHER TITLES IN THE HUMAN RESOURCE MANAGEMENT AND ORGANIZATIONAL BEHAVIOR COLLECTION

- *The 360 Degree CEO: Generating Profits While Leading and Living with Passion and Principles* by Lorraine A. Moore
- *Organizational Design in Business: A New Alternative for a Complex World* by Carrie Foster
- *Power Quotes: For Life, Business, and Leadership* by Danai Krokou
- *Magnificent Leadership: Transform Uncertainty, Transcend Circumstance, Claim the Future* by Sarah Levitt
- *Negotiating with Winning Words: Dialogue and Skills to Help You Come Out Ahead in Any Business Negotiation* by Michael Schatzki
- *Conflict First Aid: How to Stop Personality Clashes and Disputes from Damaging You or Your Organization* by Nancy Radford
- *Temperatism, Volume I: A New Way to Think About Business and Doing Good* by Carrie Foster
- *The Challenge to Be and Not to Do: How to Manage Your Career and Maximize Your Potential* by Carrie Foster
- *Slow Down to Speed Up: Lead, Succeed, and Thrive in a 24/7 World* by Liz Bywater
- *The Illusion of Inclusion: Global Inclusion, Unconscious Bias, and the Bottom Line* by Helen Turnbull
- *On All Cylinders: The Entrepreneur's Handbook* by Ron Robinson
- *Employee LEAPS: Leveraging Engagement by Applying Positive Strategies* by Kevin E. Phillips
- *Making Human Resource Technology Decisions: A Strategic Perspective* by Janet H. Marler and Sandra L. Fisher
- *Feet to the Fire: How to Exemplify And Create The Accountability That CreatesGreat Companies* by Lorraine A. Moore
- *HR Analytics and Innovations in Workforce Planning* by Tony Miller

Announcing the Business Expert Press Digital Library

Concise e-books business students need for classroom and research

This book can also be purchased in an e-book collection by your library as

- *a one-time purchase,*
- *that is owned forever,*
- *allows for simultaneous readers,*
- *has no restrictions on printing, and*
- *can be downloaded as PDFs from within the library community.*

Our digital library collections are a great solution to beat the rising cost of textbooks. E-books can be loaded into their course management systems or onto students' e-book readers.
The **Business Expert Press** digital libraries are very affordable, with no obligation to buy in future years. For more information, please visit **www.businessexpertpress.com/librarians**. To set up a trial in the United States, please email **sales@businessexpertpress.com**.

www.ingramcontent.com/pod-product-compliance
Lightning Source LLC
Chambersburg PA
CBHW071855200326
41519CB00016B/4398